First Edit...
To G...

Michael Walsh

IMPERFECTION

IMPERFECTION

The Workshop of Creation

The infant universe, 13 billion years ago
The first appearance of imperfection

It is imperfection, not perfection, that lies at the heart of our great universe.
It is the moving force behind all of nature's diversity and the key events
that have shaped our world. Without imperfection there would have been no
galaxies, no stars, no world, no living creatures and no us.

Michael J Walsh, B.E., Ph.D

authorHOUSE®

AuthorHouse™ UK Ltd.
1663 Liberty Drive
Bloomington, IN 47403 USA
www.authorhouse.co.uk
Phone: 0800.197.4150

Published by AuthorHouse 07/07/2014

ISBN: 978-1-4969-8512-5 (sc)
ISBN: 978-1-4969-8513-2 (hc)
ISBN: 978-1-4969-8514-9 (e)

DEDICATION

The book is dedicated to my son John Walsh.

He was my primary source of support and encouragement throughout the long months of preparation.

His comments and criticisms were always constructive and to the point.

TABLE OF CONTENTS

PREFACE

This book is about perfection and its opposite, imperfection. One might infer that it is about the good and the bad, the beautiful and the ugly, the wanted and the unwanted. However this would be an erroneous inference. The very reverse may in fact be true.

As we understand more about our universe, two special features stand out; the richness and beauty of nature's endless diversity and the elegance and simplicity of the laws and systems that oversee and guide this diversity. In both features, imperfection plays a leading role. It is the source of all diversity. Without it there would have been a universe of numbing uniformity. No complex organisms or structures would have emerged.

A Galaxy of Flaws
Imperfection appeared early. In the first fraction of a second after the Big Bang the infant universe inexplicably turned lumpy like sour milk. The lumps turned into galaxies, stars and worlds and the result was an uneven distribution of matter, heat and energy across space. Without the initial imperfection there would have been no galaxies, no worlds and no us. Since then, this pattern of events has repeated itself over and over again.

The living world is characterised by decay, death and rebirth. The living cell on which it is based has a life cycle full of errors, duplications, random fluctuations and accidents. Yet it has produced the wonders of nature and its infinite diversity.

Man himself is a flawed creature. Like the rest of the living world, he is subject to disease, decay and death. To constrain his wayward behaviour, society has had to invent a myriad of restraining systems such as laws, social conventions and religious guidelines. Man's mind finds itself housed in a body and environment that it does not fully comprehend and which represent to it constant threats and dangers. Its responses have given birth to the disciplines of art, science and philosophy.

Without in-built flaws, the wonderful diversity of the living and physical worlds would never have evolved. So it is time to revisit imperfection and try to unveil its many secrets. Perfection, on closer examination, plays no significant role and can lead to many paradoxes and illusions.

Perfection

The concept of perfection is an invention of the human mind which does not exist outside that domain. In a sense it is an illusion, a rainbow that we chase but never catch. We know a lot about it since the pursuit of it has been a driving force in our civilisation for over 2000 years. We can trace its origins back to ancient Greece. Since then it can claim to have given us the cathedrals of the world, the paintings of Michelangelo, the music of Mozart and the science of Newton. In the 19th century, the Age of Perfection reached its zenith. It was based on ideals of design, purpose and conformity.

As modern science reveals a universe that is not driven by purpose and design but by chance, errors, accident and other imperfections, the concept of perfection becomes more and more out of step with the deepest realities. This is increasingly reflected in our science, art and social institutions. We are now entering the Age of Imperfection.

Imperfection

Imperfection has long been hidden behind the parapets and has been treated as an unwanted fellow-traveller. Yet it is with imperfection that the real power lies. All the processes in our universe are driven by it, from the dynamics of the heavenly galaxies to the proliferation of life and even our own ever-evolving world of thought. It works by creating a cycle of disturbances and imbalances and waits for the inevitable responses that these give rise to.

Guidance

Our universe flies through space like an awesome rocket. It is built of a myriad of cosmic components that are arranged in a very particular way. It is the diversity and arrangement of components that have yielded a cosmos of such extraordinary functionality.

The rocket *universe* has a guidance system that tells each component what to do and when to act in order to help it towards its destination. It gives the impression of heading towards some destination, but we have no idea what this might be. There may in fact be no destination. What we observe may be just the universe inventing itself as it goes along.

Creation

Many theories of creation have, at their core, ideas of perfection. These must now be re-evaluated. Perfection was clearly never part of the grand design. Instead, imperfection is ubiquitous and influential.

Many may find it hard to associate imperfection with deeply-held concepts of a perfect God. Did God deliberately create a less than perfect universe? When He created the universe, was He too driven by a sense of incompleteness? Was there an unfulfilled need? Was imperfection in action even then? These are some of the deep waters into which the trail of imperfection leads us.

A New Theory

Observing the constant presence and influence of imperfection, a new theory of creation can be put forward. This envisages creation as a continuous process. It proceeds in two cycles - the cycle of kingdom creation and the cycle of kingdom evolution. Typical kingdoms are the kingdom of life and the kingdom of the human mind. There are others, some of which we do not have access to - past, present and future. A new kingdom grows out of a previous one.

During evolution, a kingdom moves over time from initial simplicity towards diversity and the building of ever more complex structures. Complex structures need a multiplicity of diverse components with which to build and it is the task of imperfection to provide these components.

It is proposed that both cycles run under the guidance of a cosmic guidance system which resides outside space and time. It consistently uses imperfection as its most effective mechanism in the creation and evolution of kingdoms. It. this sense, imperfection can be truly called the workshop of creation.

Living with Imperfection

Man has been on a search for perfection ever since the ancient Greeks set out their ideals for virtue, beauty and order. From what we now know, this may have been a misdirected search, one which has helped us to create many mental prisons for ourselves. Concepts of perfection have frequently been abused to suppress diversity and to force conformity of whole populations to certain beliefs and ideals. It is now time to accept the centrality of imperfection and to make it a cornerstone of our thinking. We will jettison many of the oppressive movements which have tried to force us into conformity while promising us unattainable utopias in return. We will experience a new sense of liberation and a freedom from futile perfection-seeking.

NOTES TO THE READER

Many of us were reared with well-inculcated ideas of order, discipline, conformity, and authority. We rarely questioned these. There was a basic assumption of well-established purpose and structure behind everything. Randomness, non-conformity and untidiness were severely frowned upon. Perfection was *in*, imperfection was *out*. Reading Aristotle and Plato reinforced all the ideas of perfection-seeking that one had been reared with.

Then one discovered modern science and slowly came the realisation that the big universe did not quite operate as one expected. Randomness, chance, uncertainty, and accident ruled. It was not meant to be like this. Perfection began to recede and imperfection stepped up to take its place. It was something of a culture shock.

Thus began my search for imperfection in all its guises. I found it everywhere, sometimes in the most unexpected places. It is not an illusion like perfection. It is real and omnipresent. I began to find that it had a strange beauty all of its own.

The idea for the book came while attending a concert of some very modern classical music in the Conservatoire in Nice. The music appeared to be chaotic and random, many miles away from the formal structures of the classical age. With the classical symphonies of the past one could almost predict what was going to happen next. This modern music was completely unpredictable. Notes and phrases appeared from just nowhere. It struck me as a metaphor for much that is happening in the modern world.

Large formal structures are crumbling everywhere. Powerful *isms* like Communism, largely based on imposed order and conformity, are faltering. In science, certainty is giving way to uncertainty and randomness. Mathematicians are seriously addressing topics such as chaos theory and randomly self-organising systems. Art sometimes takes the form of random dots on a page. Randomness and unpredictability can no longer be treated as deviations from some accepted norm. They *are* the new norm.

The need to address this development in a coherent and technically satisfying way became apparent. Searching through the literature, I could find nothing addressing the subject in a rigorous way. I felt there was need to provide a new analysis that would explain what is happening and provide a mental roadmap through it. The book thus deals with:

The implications of recent scientific findings for our world view
A new approach to imperfection, chaos, chance and unpredictability
Man's dilemma in dealing with his own imperfections
The need for re-alignment of attitudes towards the imperfect
A release from the strictures of perfectionism

The book is intended for the general reader, in particular one who is struck by the apparent randomness of the world we live in, and one who is possibly searching for a framework within which to deal with it. It covers a wide range of topics such as science, mathematics, art, philosophy, and social science. No previous knowledge of any of these areas is assumed.

Michael J. Walsh
Nice, France.
June, 2014

Chapter 1.
HELLO IMPERFECTION

Much has been written about *perfection*. It is put forward as the ultimate objective of so many of our endeavours. We are urged to seek it in sport, in the arts, in the environment in which we live, and in our personal lives and appearance. For many, the ultimate aim is to attain a state of perfection in this life and enjoy eternal perfection in the next. The search for perfection is a powerful driving force which lies behind many aspects of our lives. This may be our greatest illusion. There may be no such state as perfection.

Imperfection Revisited

We find imperfection in the natural world, in all living things, within ourselves, and deep within our innermost thoughts. It is all around us but frequently we do not want to see it. Nevertheless it is an essential part of nature and was a fundamental force in the building of our universe. The diversity of the universe has its origins in the creative power of imperfection.

From the beginning of time imperfection has been there. It is often seen as the negation of so many of the good things we strive for. We do everything we can to avoid it. Yet imperfection is an even more powerful driving force than perfection itself. Without it nothing would have happened. Perfection is a static condition, it leads to nowhere else. It is imperfection that creates the dynamic situations where things evolve and happen. A perfect universe would exist in one state only, since it cannot be improved upon. An imperfect universe creates an infinity of possible states, each with its own unique set of flaws and opportunities. Imperfection is the driving force behind change. Change is everywhere and behind it lies this hidden presence.

Recognising its importance in the scheme of things, we need look at imperfection again, perhaps in a new light. It is a fundamental part of our universe, and we must assume that it is there for some very good reason. Our task here will be to try and divine what that reason might be and how it sets out to achieve its ends. So let us focus afresh on imperfection and to ask a number of basic questions about it.

What is it?	How did it start?
Why does it exist?	How does it do its work?
What purpose does it serve?	How does it concern us?

Many Guises

Imperfection comes in many guises. It attaches itself like a spider's web to objects, people and even to ideas. Common definitions are:

> A fault or defect or failing
> A lack of completeness
> Moral weakness and defect

2

Faults and defects have an extensive vocabulary to describe their many nuances. People alone have a whole array of words exclusively devoted to their many failings. As a start, here are a few adjectives which can be applied. This list is far from complete - a full list could fill a book.

Things:	defective, faulty, broken, damaged, deformed, useless, obsolete
People:	imperfect, impaired, deficient, dysfunctional, weak, failed, dangerous
Ideas:	erroneous, false, strange, twisted, unfinished, unworkable, incomplete
Systems:	oppressive, inefficient, chaotic, unresponsive, expensive
The "Un's"	uncertain, unusual, unsightly, untrue, unwell, unwise, unthinkable
The "Im's"	immature, immoral, implausible, impolite, impotent, improper
The "In's"	incomplete, inaccurate, inadequate, inane, incoherent, incorrect

A very useful word is *flawed.* It applies to everything. Everything has a flaw, no matter how well hidden.

Not-knowing is to the human mind one of the greatest flaws. From very early times man has battled with special kinds of flaws - the unknown, the unpredictable, the misunderstood, the hidden and the mysterious. These his intelligence cannot tolerate for very long. They represent threats to him. The battle against them lies at the very root of his art, science, social systems, philosophy and religion. These are driven by an overwhelming need-to-know and understand.

3

Man is frequently portrayed as a fallen creature, full of moral weaknesses and defects. Left to himself, he can be selfish, cruel, unjust, destructive, untrustworthy and many other unpleasant things. To keep him in check, innumerable control systems have been invented. A vast library would be needed to house all the counter measures invented by legislators, teachers and religious leaders. These do not cure human weaknesses and defects but at least they put a ring fence around them.

A Random Universe

We have come to think that the universe works like an expensive Swiss watch. It ticks along with precision and elegance. Each wheel has its purpose and performs it precisely. We feel that if we can finally understand the function of every little wheel, we will have mastered the grand design of the universe.

In reality this is a false idea. The universe operates by chance and its successes have come about by sheer fluke. It has the huge advantage that most of its failures are buried in history. It enjoys the reverse of the adage: *The evil that men do lives after them. The good they do is oft interred with their bones*[1]. What we see of nature is only its successes. Its failures are lost in prehistory. It may have made millions of false starts over billions of years to reach success. But this does not matter. It is patient. It has plenty of time to play with.

We may not like this randomness, but each new discovery in science confirms it. God did not make the world like a Swiss watch. He

---

[1]   **Shakespeare**, 1564-1616. *Julius Caesar*...Marc Anthony at Caesar's grave

made it more like a game of lottery. Our new model of the universe tends to be more and more based on imperfection, accident, and randomness. In its own way, this new vision of creation is just as beautiful a concept as the old one. It just takes a while to get used to it.

It's not that I believe everything happens for a reason. It's just that…
I just think that some things are meant to be broken. Imperfect.
Chaotic. It's the universe's way of providing contrast, you know.
There have to be a few holes in the road. Its how life is.

\- Sarah Dessen[2]

---

[2] **Sarah Dessen**, American Writer, b. 1970 Illinois, *The Truth About Forever*, www. sarahdessen.com

Chapter 2.
BYE-BYE PERFECTION

Perfection often seems like a kind of magnet that draws us towards it, and makes us turn our backs on imperfection. Intuitively we feel that we know what perfection is, but like the rainbow, the closer we come to it, the further it recedes from us. Like the foot of the rainbow, there is no such place as perfection. We may have spent thousands of years chasing rainbows.

> *Out of perfection nothing can be made. Every process involves breaking something up.*
>
> - Joseph Campbell[3]

The oldest definition of perfection goes back to Aristotle [4]. In his book *Delta* of the *Metaphysics*, he gives three meanings of the term, distinguishing three shades of the concept:

---

[3] Joseph John **Campbell,** 1904-1978. N.Y. / Hawaii Writer/Mythologist. *The Hero with a Thousand Faces*

[4] **Aristotle**, Greek Philosopher, 384–322 BC, student of Plato and teacher of Alexander the Great.

That is perfect:

1. which is complete — which contains all the requisite parts;
2. which is so good that nothing of the kind could be better;
3. which has attained its purpose.

This definition has been debated for centuries. Thomas Aquinas[5] in his *Summa Theologica* saw in it a twofold perfection - perfection in *substance,* when a thing is perfect in itself, and perfection in *purpose*, when it perfectly serves its purpose.

The distinction between perfection and excellence has also been endlessly debated. Excellence implies comparison - it is the best of many. Perfection on the other hand involves no comparison. If something is deemed perfect, then it is deemed so in itself without comparison to other things. Leibniz[6], who thought much about perfection, held the world to be the best of all possible worlds, but did not claim that it was perfect. It was therefore excellent but not perfect.

The first two lines of the definition, perfection in substance, relate mostly to people's perception. We can build what we think is the perfect house. It will be complete, nothing will be missing. We cannot think of anything that could be better. However our personal needs and circumstances change with time and what was once deemed perfect now displays many flaws. This kind of perfection is thus subjective and ephemeral. It does not have any solid grounding.

---

[5]   Thomas **Aquinas**, 1225–1274, Sicily. Philosopher/Theologian,

[6]   Gottfried Wilhelm von **Leibnitz**, 1646-1716, Leipzig/Hannover. German Mathematician/Philosopher,

Nature goes for the third definition. A beautiful bird in flight is a good example of perfect fitness for purpose. Its size, shape, bone structure and wing shape are all perfectly tuned to the task of flying. Every feather has a function. Its beauty in our eyes comes from this perfect matching of need and design. This kind of perfection appears to have a more solid basis. But the design needs constant adaptation to meet changes in habitat or food supply, so this kind of perfection is a moving target. It has no absolute existence.

Perfection is closely linked to:

        beauty.........the basis of most of our art

        elegance... a quality prized in fashion but also by scientists and mathematicians

        order.......... the opposite of chaos and disorder

        heaven ......a place where all imperfections are finally resolved

Countless volumes have been written attempting to answer the question: *What is beauty?* We are probably no nearer an answer than Plato[7], who was one of the first to tackle this question 2500 years ago. Many kinds of beauty are just fashion. A visit to an art gallery will show how much the vision of perfect female beauty has changed over the years. Rubens liked his beauties luscious and rotund. Nowadays we like them skeleton-thin.

Scientists, trying to model the behaviour of the world around them, often come up with beautiful equations. They expect the equations on which the world was constructed to be elegant, not clumsy looking.

---

[7]   **Plato**, 427-347 BCE, Athens. Greek Philosopher/Mathematician, Student of Socrates.

By elegance they mean a kind of fitness for purpose, somewhat akin to the bird in flight - the behaviour of the equation matches perfectly the behaviour of the phenomenon it was designed to model. But even the greatest scientific theories decay over time, so here the perfection is again transitory.

We enjoy seeing order in our world. When we visit the garden of some stately mansion, we marvel at its precision. The grass is cut every day to a precise height. There is not a weed in sight. The flower beds are models of geometric precision. The flowers are placed so that their colours match all the year round. All of this gives us a nice, warm feeling. Here at least, man is the master of unruly nature. Here he is in control.

Many religions define heaven as the place where true perfection is finally attained. We will have *thrown off the mortal coil* [8] and escaped from all the tribulations of this imperfect world. However there are so many conflicting views as to what heaven really is that uncertainty still prevails, and uncertainty is a serious flaw in any concept.

So absolute perfection is very hard to pin down. If perfection contains the seeds of its own decay, then quite simply it is not perfection. The best we can say about it is that it represents something whose flaws have not yet become apparent.

Origins

The attainment of perfection has been the aspiration of western societies for over 2000 years. Where does this aspiration come

---

[8]   **Shakespeare**, *Hamlet*

from? Is it an inescapable part of being human or is it just a language we have learned from childhood?

The Egyptians thought that God made the world from a heap of stones, imposing order and shape on them. To replicate creation, they built the pyramids, also of stones and beautifully ordered. The ancient Greeks sought perfection in the human form, and their many magnificent sculptures are testimony to their quest.

Archimedes[9] concluded that behind the observable world was a perfect harmony. Simple mathematical laws lay behind every phenomenon. In his bath, he wondered why the sponge floated on the water, partly submerged, and not sinking. He hit on the famous law - a floating object sinks until it has displaced its own weight of water. He ran into the street, naked, shouting *Eureka. Eureka* We have been searching for the same harmony ever since and shouting *Eureka* when we find the answer.

Euclid[10] wrote his beautiful 13 books of geometry, *The Elements*, around 300BCE. In these, he set out with precision a complete description of the space we live in. To this day children are taught his ideas of perfect circles, squares and parallel lines. Perhaps Euclid is to blame when we try to impose these perfect shapes on a nature that knows nothing about such things.

---

[9]   **Archimedes**, 287-212BCE, Syracuse Sicily. Greek mathematician/inventor/ astronomer,

[10]   **Euclid**, 330-260 BCE. Greek mathematician, often referred to as the "Father of Geometry".

The pursuit of personal perfection has been closely linked with belief in the existence of the human soul. Early Persian and Greek philosophers believed that humans possess a dual nature - the body, which can be a source of evil, and the soul, the source of goodness. The body was believed to be the tomb of the soul. By leading a good and pure life, the soul might eventually escape the body and fully realise its divine nature. Elements of these beliefs found their way into the religions emanating from the eastern Mediterranean - Christianity, Judaism and Islam. Since then, thousands of great thinkers, teachers and prophets have expounded the philosophy of personal perfection.

Plato

Plato is important in the context of this book. He associated the observed world with *imperfection*, and the world of the human intellect with *perfection*. He held that the real world was but a flawed mimic of the perfect world which the intellect has inherited and has access to. His ideas of perfection have had a profound effect even to this day.

Plato remains to this day one of the world's most widely read philosophers. He was a student of Socrates and he taught Aristotle. In Athens he founded the Academy, the first institution of higher learning in the western world. His writings cover philosophy, logic, ethics, rhetoric, religion and mathematics.

Plato was particularly interested in mathematics and may have studied under Euclid. He was well aware of the mysterious power of mathematics to model the physical world, as Euclid had done. He was one of the first philosophers to study the natural world and the way that we interpret it within our minds. He addressed topics of profound interest such as reality, abstraction, existence and perfection.

Theory of Forms

Plato developed his *Theory of Forms* or Universals around 350BC. Its key elements are:

Forms

Two distinct levels of reality exist, the visible world we inhabit and the abstract world of Forms that exists elsewhere. Behind ever object (such as a tree) and every concept (such as Justice) there lies an unseen reality – a Form. There is a Form of Tree and a Form of Justice. We recognise objects and concepts because of their resemblance to their Forms. Forms possess the highest and most fundamental kind of reality. They are eternal and unchanging. We cannot have contact with Forms with our senses. We can only make contact with them through our intellect.

The World

Nature is flawed, an approximation to the perfect world of Forms. Ordinary objects are imperfect and changeable, but they faintly mimic the perfect and immutable Forms. The body and its passions are rooted in the physical world, while the mind and body belong to the ideal world. This is man's dual nature. In the world of changing appearances we may catch a glimpse of perfection, but it will always fade. It is just a pointer to the perfect beauty of the eternal.

The Locus

Forms exist independently of the sensible world. They exist in the Locus, which is outside space and time and is eternal. In the Locus there is an infinite volume of absolute truths to which the mind has access.

The Mind and Soul

We are born with innate knowledge of the Forms. Our souls had contact with the Locus before becoming incarnate in the human body at birth. Therefore our souls are immortal. We need only be reminded of the Forms through study and education. This is known as the doctrine of recollection.

The world of Forms can be understood only by philosophers and those who seek knowledge. Abstraction is superior to the world of the senses. The best human life is one that strives to understand and imitate the Forms as closely as possible.

Perfection

The essential element of Platonic Forms is *perfection*. They represent a perfection that the material world can only mimic and approximate to.

> *The Platonic idealist is by nature so wedded to perfection that he sees in everything not the reality but the faultless ideal which reality suggests and misses.*
>
> - George Santayana, *Egotism in German Philosophy.*

Goodness

There is a Form of Good which is superior to all other Forms. Our souls have access to this Form.

An Illusion?

Not all agree with Plato's analysis. Bertrand Russell[11] called concepts such that of a tree *ephemeral chimera of the mind.*

Plato took the triangle as an example of a Form. We can easily carry the concept of a perfect triangle in our heads. We can draw a triangle with various degrees of precision. But no matter how precisely we draw it, there will be tiny flaws. Under a high-resolution magnifying glass we will easily see them. The drawing is thus a poor mimic of the perfect image we had in our heads. Plato proposed that this perfect image is something absolute and eternal, existing even outside our physical universe.

However this may be an illusion. We create the image of a triangle by using information stored in our memories. We have memorised the rules for constructing a triangle ever since our first encounter with Euclid. Applying these rules we create the internal image – dynamically, on-the-fly. There is no need for the mind to store any actual image of a perfect triangle (there could be thousands of them) since it can reconstruct a new one in a fraction of a second. To its author, the created image is complete. He cannot think of anything better, and it completely fulfils his purposes. This is precisely Aristotle's definition of perfection. So the image appears perfect to the author. Even if he has a confused knowledge of Euclid and applies the wrong rules, the result will still appear perfect to him. By definition, it cannot appear other than *perfect*. The image has been specifically constructed to represent the stored rules, even if these are flawed. It is self-referential, in that it is created by the mind to satisfy itself,

---

[11] Bertrand **Russell**, 1872 – 1970. British mathematician/philosopher,

without the intervention of any external criteria. It is judgmental, in that it relies for completeness on the judgment of its own creator.

Perfection in the Platonic sense may thus be an illusion, being a spinoff from the internal mechanisms that we use to create our mental images.

Infinity

The concept of perfection has much in common with that of infinity.

The idea of infinity has plagued mathematics ever since the time of Euclid. If we think of infinity as an extremely large number, what happens when we add 1 to this number? We get a new infinity. If we can imagine an infinitely long line, we can always add one meter to it and we get a new infinity. Repeating steps such as these, we can arrive at an infinite number of infinities which is absurd.

Euclid defined parallel lines as two lines that meet at infinity. Nobody has ever been able to define exactly where that is. Yet it is a cornerstone of all Euclid's' 13 books of geometry. If this idea is flawed, then the entire 13 books are also flawed. Even modern mathematics is not immune as it too has been proven to lead to unexpected paradoxes.

To Aristotle, *perfect* meant *complete* - there is nothing to add or subtract. The ancient philosopher Empedocles[12] argued that if perfection cannot be improved on, then this is in itself a flaw. If

---

[12]   **Empedocles**, ca. 490–430BCE. Agrigentum, Sicily. Greek Philosopher,

the world were perfect, it could not improve and so would lack *true perfection*, which depends on progress. To Empedocles, perfection depends on imperfection since the latter possesses the potential for development and for acquiring new characteristics. This view parallels the baroque esthetic of Marin Mersenne[13] that the perfection of a work of art consists in its forcing the recipient to be active—to complement the art work by an effort of mind and imagination. We thus arrive at the paradox that perfection requires some degree of imperfection.

A good example of the perfection paradox arises in the world of electronics. The transistor has revolutionised the field of electronics, and is present in our radios, televisions, phones and electronic watches. It is a made from a semiconductor material such as silicon. Semiconductor materials are useful because their behaviour can be easily manipulated by the addition of impurities, known as doping. Thus an imperfection, in the form of contaminants, is a prerequisite for the production of semiconductors. The solution to this apparent paradox lies in Aquinas' distinction between the two concepts of perfection: that of *substance* and that of *utility*. The semi-conductor requires imperfection in substance in order to achieve functional perfection.

Paradoxes

If we consider the three big entities of creation - God, man and nature - in terms of perfection and imperfection we arrive at many paradoxes. Here are a few:

---

[13] Marin **Mersenne**, 1588–1648. French theologian/philosopher/mathematician,

God

Many religions ascribe perfection in all its manifestations to God. He is the ultimate symbol of perfection. But if he created the universe and man, then he must have felt that was something missing and he had to put it right. Therefore, by Aristotle's definition, he could not have been perfect.

God/World

God is perfect. Yet he created a world that at fundamental level is constructed around imperfection. Why did he choose imperfection as the principal driving force?

Man/Nature

Man was shaped by nature and his entire existence depends on it. Yet his deepest desire is to distance himself from nature and to ultimately escape altogether from its constraints – illness, adversity and death. This paradox lies at the root of so many of his inner conflicts.

Nature

The mathematical laws that lie behind nature are often very beautiful and have the sheen of perfection. Perhaps Plato was right. Nature is much less perfect than the mathematical models of it which man creates in his head.

Man

Man, at intellectual level, would like nature to conform to his ideas of order and structure, but nature often works to a different set of rules. Plato held that the real world was but a flawed mimic of the perfect world of the intellect. So from the beginning, there appears an apparent mismatch between the two realities.

Excellence

The crux with all these paradoxes is the use of the word *perfection*. If we substitute it with the word excellence, then most of the paradoxes disappear. Mathematicians try strenuously to avoid using the term *infinity,* as it can yield absurd results when they use it in their equations - you cannot multiply or divide infinity by anything. Perhaps we should equally strenuously avoid using the word *perfection*. We should instead talk about excellence. To differentiate God, we could assign to him the term super-excellence.

For thousands of years, perfection has been a foundation stone of our education, science, religion and endeavours. Yet perfection is an illusion. It has no absolute existence. It is at best judgmental and self-referential and leads to many strange paradoxes. With recent developments in science, its flaws have begun to appear.

The Reality

Imperfection has much better credentials to be considered as something absolute. With it we can account for everything that has happened in the last 13 billion years. It has a sound theoretical basis[14], much sounder that perfection. It does not suffer from the same paradoxes. So let's restore it to its rightful place – it is a pre-requisite for much that has happened in our universe.

---

[14]   Its theoretical basis will be addressed in Chapter 9.

The following chapters will examine in some detail the physical world, the living world and the world of man, addressing the unique flaws that characterise each world and identifying the chain reaction of responses that these flaws invoke. Slowly the hidden power of imperfection will be discovered.

Chapter 3.
THE NATURAL WORLD

In nature, nothing is perfect and everything is perfect.
Trees can be contorted, bent in weird ways, and they're
still beautiful."

- Alice Walker[15]

The natural world has an aura of perfection. When we look at the night sky we envy the calmness and serenity it exudes. The moon follows its appointed path. The planets rotate harmoniously in their appointed orbits. The stars twinkle as they have done for millions of years. There is order and predictability about it all. As we see the serenity of the night sky, we often compare it with the turbulence and chaos of our daily lives, and wish we could somehow achieve the same tranquillity.

Of course things are not really like that at all. The heavens are a very turbulent and violent place. There is death, birth, destruction and catastrophe up there as well as here. It just happens so slowly that we do not notice it. A million years is a short time in the life of

---

[15]   Alice **Walker**, b.1944 Georgia. African American writer, Pulitzer prize for fiction 1982.

the cosmos. Our thoughts turn naturally to the question of the origins and purpose of this wonderful display in the heavens.

What is the moon? What is the stars? - Joxer Daly[16]

In addition to Joxer Daly, the greatest philosophers and scientists have turned their minds to such questions.

> Is the world a beautifully thought-out machine, obeying elegant timeless laws?
> Or is its appearance of perfection an illusion?
> Could it have happened by accident?
> Was our small world designed specifically for us?
> Or is our presence here just another cosmic accident?
> Is the universe, at its most fundamental level, driven by perfection or imperfection?

There are conflicting schools of thought on these big questions. Here will be explored the thesis that imperfection and its consequences lie behind most of what we observe of the physical world.

Imperfection Appears

Imperfection made its appearance at an early stage in the history of the universe. It made its entrance very shortly after the Big Bang. Cosmologists can put a fairly accurate time on its arrival as their mathematical models enable them to roll back the expansion of the universe to within a fraction of a second of the Big Bang.

---

[16]   Sean **O'Casey**,1880-1964, Irish playwright, *The Plough and the Stars, 1926*

Immediately after the Big Bang, the entire universe was astonishingly small. It measured less than a millionth of a centimetre across. All its subsequent power and energy were concentrated into this tiny space. It was made up of radiation at an unimaginably high temperature. It was perfectly uniform across. Scientists use the word *smooth* to describe it.

The infant universe immediately began an explosive expansion phase, expanding at many times the speed of light. This phase, called inflation, lasted for only a fraction of a second. When it was completed, the initial smoothness was lost and the universe was now lumpy. Imperfection had arrived.

NASA image of the infant universe

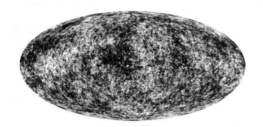

Scientists surmised that the inflation process would leave behind a footprint of radiation in the sky. Sensational proof of this was achieved just a few years ago. NASA in 1995 began the WMAP project[17] which succeeded in mapping the traces of background radiation left behind. The image is shown above. It gives an astonishing picture of what the universe looked like 13 billion years ago, very shortly after its birth. It confirms the lumpiness of the early universe. The image

---

[17] *The detailed, all-sky picture of the infant universe was created from seven years of WMAP data. The image reveals 13.7 billion-year-old temperature fluctuations that correspond to the seeds that grew to become the galaxies. Image courtesy of Science Team NASA / WMAP (Wilkinson Microwave Anisotrophy Probe)*

shows tiny temperature fluctuations of the order of ±.05 degrees. These fluctuations may appear trivial but they were to be of crucial importance. They were the seeds that grew to become the galaxies. Without them there would not have developed any galaxies, stars or worlds. The universe would be a boringly featureless place.

Scientists are uncertain as to the source of these early fluctuations. Some believe they may have arisen as a result of small temporary perturbations allowed for under modern quantum theory[18].

Lee Smolin[19] has written:

> *The theory that structure forms from small perturbations in an otherwise symmetric universe may be true in outline, but even if it is true it is incomplete. There must be some good reason why a universe that starts off as symmetrical and simple ends up developing such complexity, and if we are honest, we must admit that we do not yet know what it is.*

The exact scientific reasons need not concern us here, but the fact that the birth of the universe was driven by a process that intrinsically created random fluctuations and unevenness is of particular significance. Early imperfection created the seeds from which grew all the cosmic structures - galaxies, stars and worlds like ours.

---

[18] Discussed later in this Chapter

[19] Lee **Smolin,** American theoretical physicist/cosmologist, *The Life of the Cosmos,*1997

A Universe of Life

Ours is a universe of life; its initial setup made it so. The laws that govern it seem specifically designed to create habitats where life could develop.

Behind these laws are fundamental constants that determine exactly how matter in the universe is formed and behaves. These constants include the actual values selected for the masses of the fundamental particles such as the electron and the proton, the values of their electric charges, the strength of the fundamental forces such as gravity, etc. These had to be selected to an incredible degree of precision to yield a universe such as ours. Their values are very extraordinary and the minutest variation in any one of them would have resulted in a very different universe, almost certainly one where life as we know it could not develop. Scientists know this because they can now build computer models of the early universe and can experiment at will with different combinations and values for these parameters and laws.

A Multiverse

Scientists, faced with explaining away the extraordinary precision and uniqueness of the startup parameters of our universe, propose the existence of millions of universes. Each would have different startup parameters and fundamental laws, perhaps inherited from a previous universe. Most of the universes would not support life as we know it. We just happen to live the one (perhaps the only one) that can support life.

There are a number of variations of the multiverse theory. One interesting theory comes from Lee Smolin. It indicates an element of randomness in the inherited laws of nature and in the start-up parameters. It thus provides one possible explanation as to how these extraordinary start-up conditions were arrived at in the first place.

> There are millions of universes connected as in a family tree. A universe can give birth to another universe, in a process involving black holes in space (these arise in extreme situations predicted by the theory of relativity). Each new universe has characteristics slightly different from its parent, such as its fundamental equations and startup parameters. The variations in these characteristics are small but completely random. They are necessary to ensure that the child is not a perfect replica of the parent. Afterwards a process of natural selection takes place somewhat like what occurs in biological evolution, the criterion for success here being the ability to create more black holes and thus perpetuate the dynasty. The conditions for the creation of black holes and the conditions necessary for the support of life are closely related so, as the probability of more black holes increases, so also does the probability of life. After many millions of iterations of the creation cycle, the right combination for the lock was eventually found and here we are!

In this theory, universes behave much like a living organism and go through similar cycles of birth, evolution and death.

Setting up the World

The early perturbations resulted in an uneven distribution of matter, energy and heat across the universe. Matter clumped together into galaxies. Stars were formed whose internal nuclear reactions created nodes of intense heat. Different chemical elements appeared in different places. Then somehow about 4.5 billion years ago, our world appeared. It was very unique. It was a world that could support life. For this to happen, an extraordinary set of conditions was required:

The sun had to be of the right size.

The earth had to be just the right distance from the sun for it to have a moderate temperature.

The tilt of its axis of rotation was required to yield the seasons.

It had to contain the right elements such as water, carbon and hydrogen.

It had to have an atmosphere that would filter out dangerous radiation from space.

Scientists marvel at the chain of coincidences that were necessary for intelligent life to have developed on earth. Any minute variation of any of the key factors would have precluded life. All the factors are accidental, and their coincidence is so unique that it is highly improbable, but not impossible, that it could be replicated elsewhere in the universe to yield the same result – intelligent life.

Scientists are now discovering thousands of planets such as ours, orbiting other stars in the heavens. Some, like Mars, may have supported a rudimentary form of life in the past, but as yet no clues of intelligent life have been found. Giant radio telescopes constantly scan the skies, waiting for that first tell-tale signal from outer space.

The Laws of Nature

It is the laws of nature that guide and govern the natural world. It is they that determine the dynamics of all things. Everything from particles to galaxies must obey their rule. They are effectively the software that guides the hardware of the universe. Many mysteries surround these laws.

Where did they come from? Where do they reside?

How are material things aware of them and know how to obey them?

How do we humans discover them? Do we discover them correctly?

Are the laws of science we derive just poor mimics of the real laws?

Why is mathematics so powerful in modelling the universe?

What sort of world views emerge from these laws?

Can we ever discover one universal law explaining all creation?

What world view can we derive from these laws?

To many of these questions there are no definitive answers. Modern science has discovered advanced theories that reach deeper and deeper into the behaviour of the universe, but the philosophic questions that lie behind this behaviour remain as elusive as ever.

In Chapter 10, an attempt will be made to provide an entirely new framework within which these questions can be debated. It consists of a proposed cosmic operating system that has imperfection at its heart. Some of the important topics are addressed below.

Awareness

How are material things aware of the laws of nature and how do they know how to respond to them? Etienne Klein has written as follows[20]:

> Imagine two electrons, the first two particles of the universe. They carry two electric charges of the same sign. They experience an electric force that drives them apart, the more so the closer they are. It is the law of electromagnetism at work. But how do they know the physical law that humans have to learn in college? Is it inscribed in the depths of their being since their formation? Have they remembered them by heart? Can they decrypt them from a distance from some great notice board of the universe? Are they obeying instructions that come from outside the world? Or are they in negotiation with the Universe as to how best electrically charged particles should behave themselves? I may seem to be not serious, but the nature of the laws of physics remains a true question of metaphysics

The Laws of Science

Science is man's attempt to unveil the laws of Nature. While the latter in their native form are totally inaccessible to the human mind, science can infer much about them by studying and analysing their consequences. Models can be drawn up which enable the future behaviour of nature to be predicted with extraordinary precision.

Current scientific theories fall into two main categories – Classical Science and Quantum Theory.

---

[20]   Etienne **Klein**, French Physicist. GEO Savoir, No.3, March-April 2012.

Classical Science

Classical science is considered to have started with *Galileo*[21]. He is often called the father of modern physics and astronomy. He made improvements to the telescope and used it to make many important discoveries about the planets and the solar system. He advocated heliocentrism, the belief that the sun is the centre of the solar system. In addition he laid the foundations for the sciences of dynamics, falling bodies, strength of materials and tides.

With Isaac Newton[22], science took its next giant leap forward. Newton was born one year after Galileo's death. To many he is the greatest scientist who ever lived. His book *Principia Mathematica* (1687) is often called the single-most influential book in physics. It presented the Law of Gravitation which enabled for the first time the motion of the planets to be calculated with precision and it united the heavens and the earth under the same physical laws. Newton also made important contributions to optics, dynamics and mathematics. He was co-inventor with Leibnitz of the calculus, one of the most powerful mathematical tools available to physicists.

In 1908 Einstein[23] published his Theory of Relativity. In many ways it overturned Newton's concept of the universe. It proposed that time, space and distance were not absolute, but relative, and that the only constant was the speed of light. The new concept of *spacetime* was born – a model combining space and time into a single four-dimensional continuum, replacing Euclid's well-established

---

[21] **Galileo Galilei,** 1564-1642, Florence Italy. Italian astronomer and physicist

[22] Sir Isaac **Newton,**1642-1727, English physicist/mathematician/astronomer,

[23] Albert **Einstein,** 1955-1979, German Physicist. b.Ulm, Germany, d. Princeton, USA

three-dimensional model of space. Einstein derived the famous equation **E=mc²**, which indicates that matter (m) is the equivalent of vast amounts of stored energy (E). This equation led to the development of nuclear energy and the atomic bomb.

Thermodynamics

This is a branch of classical science concerned with the transfer of heat and energy across systems. It laws are considered as very fundamental as most other laws of physics cans be derived from them.

A fundamental part of thermodynamics is the concept of entropy. It is used by scientists as a measure of disorder in any system. As the universe expands, it descends from order into disorder. The heat, initially concentrated in localised pockets, gets diffused across the system and is no longer available to do useful work such as heating our planet. The final state of the universe is called its heat death. Then a low uniform temperature will have been reached everywhere. All movement and heat exchange will cease. The universe will have descended into a state of maximum disorder, i.e. maximum entropy). The term entropy, although originating in thermodynamics, has found many applications outside its original field. Some definitions that are highly relevant to our purposes are:

A measure of disorder or randomness in a closed system.

A measure of the loss of information in a transmitted message.

Inevitable and steady deterioration in a system or society

It is easy to see that entropy is also a measure of imperfection. Its key words such as randomness, loss of information and deterioration are all descriptors of imperfection. So imperfection is built into this most fundamental of laws.

Quantum Theory

Classical physics explains matter and energy on a scale familiar to human experience. Towards the end of the 19th century, scientists dealing with the fundamental particles of which matter is made up – electrons, protons, photons - discovered phenomena that classical science could not explain. A new theory was needed.

Quantum Theory was developed to explain physical behaviour at molecular, atomic and sub-atomic level. It is about the nature of matter.

Max Planck[24] is credited with the first formulation of the theory, while Werner Heisenberg[25] derived one of its most eminent laws, the Uncertainty Principle. This relates to how we affect a particle we are trying to measure. By just observing a particle, we change its behaviour so we can never be sure of its original state. For example, the more precisely the position of a particle is determined, the less precisely its momentum can be determined, and vice versa.

The defining characteristic of Quantum Theory is that it is statistical in nature. The fundamental particles behave randomly and precise predictions about their behaviour cannot be made. Only probabilities

---

[24] Max **Planck**, 1858-1947. German Physicist, b. Kiel, Nobel Prize for Physics 1918

[25] Werner Karl *Heisenberg*, 1901-1976. *German Physicist*, one of the founders of quantum theory

can be calculated. Often the simple rules of cause and effect, a cornerstone of classical science, are often breached.

Einstein's Theory of Relativity is about the largest things in the universe. Quantum Theory is about the smallest. The two theories are not at all compatible and scientists conclude that at least one of them must be wrong. Nevertheless quantum theory provides formidable explanations as to the behaviour of matter at its tiniest level.

Decay

The physical laws that govern the universe are considered to be something perfect, eternal and immutable. They do not decay. Material things must have first-hand access to these laws as they are obviously able to read them, decode them and carry out their instructions. Man's intellect has only second-hand access to the laws in their native form.

Science proceeds by observing the behaviour of nature and guessing what its hidden laws might be. It tries to model this behaviour through scientific theories and mathematical models. It has no guarantee that its models are exact representations. They may be approximations and, with the passage of time, imperfections may emerge making it necessary to start over again.

Scientific theories go through life cycles very similar to that of living things – growth, flowering, decay, death and rebirth. History tells us that the greatest theories in time develop flaws. Newton's Law of Gravitation stood for centuries but eventually began to show some imperfections. It was eventually superseded by Einstein's Theory of Relativity. This in turn has its own imperfections, and many scientists are currently working intensively to find its replacement. A theory with a flaw is no longer perfect, using Aristotle's criterion of perfection. The quest for its replacement inexorably follows, as science cannot long tolerate a theory that appears less than perfect.

> *No amount of experimentation can ever prove me right; a single experiment can prove me wrong.* - Einstein

> *Science, like life, feeds on its own decay. New facts burst old rules; then newly divined conceptions bind old and new together into a reconciling law.*
>
> - William James[26]

The laws of nature may be absolute, but our mimic of them in the form of scientific theories cannot lay a similar claim to being absolute. Einstein was well aware of this.

Roger Penrose[27]

In his monumental book *The Road to Reality*, Robert Penrose has summarised all the known laws of physics in a single volume. It covers everything from the smallest particles to intergalactic space. One is tempted to ask: *Is there an equivalent great volume written*

---

[26] William **James** (1842-1910) American philosopher/psychologist.

[27] Sir Roger **Penrose** (1931-). English mathematician, physicist and philosopher of science. University of Oxford. *The Road to Reality; A Complete Guide to the Laws of the Universe, 2007*

somewhere in the skies? If so, Roger Penrose would certainly love to be able to read it!

World Views

The world of quantum mechanics is based on *randomness* and chance, while the world of much of classical science is based on *determinism*. These represent two very different and incompatible world views. Which is the real world?

Determinism

Determinism can be defined as the philosophical doctrine that all events including human actions and choices are fully determined by preceding events and states of affairs. In science it relates to order and predictability within natural phenomena. Behind every phenomenon there is an assumption of purpose and design. The design is likely to be some beautiful mathematical equation which predetermines exactly how something behaves - now, in the past and into the indefinite future. Once the laws that lie behind a phenomenon are known, it is easy to predict its future behaviour.

If a stone is dropped from the top of a high building, one can calculate precisely the time it will take to fall and the final speed it will attain. Given the height of the building and the known value of the acceleration due to gravity, there is a neat equation in mechanics which yields the desired results. If a ball is thrown in the air, there is an equation to calculate how high it will rise and how far it will travel before it hits the ground. It is first necessary to know the speed and angle at which the ball was thrown. An equation can describe how the ball behaves, but it cannot tell who threw the ball or why.

Determinism received a huge boost from Newton's Law of Gravitation which enabled the motion of the planets to be modeled and predicted with precision. The assumption was that similar elegant laws lay behind every phenomenon, and the race to find such laws began. Such was Newton's influence that this view of the world was called after him, Newtonian. Even when Newton's laws were superseded centuries later by the theory of relativity, the Newtonian view still held. Einstein was a confirmed Newtonian. Many scientists are still searching for the one integrated mathematical theory that will explain everything. Some feel they are getting closer and closer. Others feel that it is an exercise doomed to failure.

The earliest critic of the cult of determinism was Leibnitz. (He was a contemporary of Newton and independently invented the calculus at the same time as Newton). He argued that a Newtonian world implied that some things (equations, design etc) existed outside the universe and somehow pre-dated it. If these somethings existed outside of our universe, then they belonged to some bigger universe, which in turn required explanation. He argued that solutions must be found within the confines of the present universe without having to invoke something from outside. He proved it was impossible for determinism to find solutions within this constraint. His world view is now called Leibnitzian.

Randomness

The weather is an example of a random system. It is impossible to predict the weather beyond the immediate future and even then it often proves wrong. It obviously obeys some laws but these are so complex and the starting conditions so difficult to determine that any kind of long-range forecasting is hazardous.

The elementary particles that make up the atom, such as electrons and protons, do not obey deterministic laws. Their behaviour is quite random and cannot be predicted with any degree of precision. Science has had to develop a novel theory to deal with them –quantum theory. With its development, modern science started to move further and further away from the Newtonian world view. Ideas of randomness, probability and chance began to move centre-stage.

The laws of classical science, with their precise modeling of actual phenomena, lead one to believe that the universe is essentially deterministic. After all one can predict the exact position of the earth with relation to the sun one thousand years from now. However these laws are response mechanisms and it is easy to lose sight of what exactly they are responding to.

The perturbations in the early universe resulted in an uneven distribution of matter and energy across the universe. It is to these imbalances that the laws of nature are responding to. Without them they would have had nothing to work on. In a totally smooth universe they would have had no purpose. So what is observed is the *determinate* responding to the *indeterminate*. The indeterminate came first.

Mathematics

Mathematicians studying nature often create mathematical models of it and manipulate these models using the very powerful toolkit available to them. These models are very important in physics where theories are almost invariably expressed using mathematical models. The models are used to create predictions of behaviour which are then tested by experimental measurements. They are refined or discarded according to the results.

One of the mysterious powers of mathematics is that it enables scientists to extrapolate to situations and data way beyond those for which the model was initially designed. Many important discoveries have been predicted by mathematics, such as the presence of black holes in space or the existence of anti-matter and anti-particles. Mathematics demanded that these had to exist in order to maintain the integrity of its equations. When searched for, they were found to be there exactly as predicted.

In contemplating the mysterious way in which nature obeys elegant mathematical laws thought up by the human mind, Plato drew a triangle as follows:

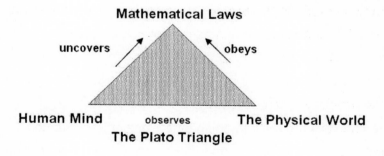

The Plato Triangle

The triangle illustrates the three major players:

Mathematical Laws:

The physical world is based on mathematical laws. These laws exist in the Locus, independent of the universe and of man. They laws are timeless and unchanging. They represent true perfection.

The Physical World
This is but a flawed mimic of the perfect world inscribed in the Locus.

The Human Mind
The human mind has access to the Locus, using the intellect, in some mysterious way. The resulting concepts in the human mind are therefore perfect also.

Experimental science did not exist in Plato's day. He therefore did not envisage laws of science that were models based on observation of the physical world and thus mimics of a mimic. He dismissed art in exactly these terms deeming it a flawed representation of a flawed reality and thus doubly flawed. Nevertheless his triangle and the relationships it depicts remain as mysterious as ever.

A Theory of Everything
Many scientists are still searching for the one super-equation that will explain the whole universe and its origins. (If found, someone has remarked that it should be concise enough to fit on a tee-shirt. After all Einstein's famous equation **E=mc²** has achieved this distinction!). Imagine that someone has found this one super-equation, the so-called theory of everything (TOE) Imagine it to be something as undistinguished as this:

$$G = 3 + 5x + 7Y^2$$

The values 3, 5 and 7 represent the constants of the equation. For a TOE, they stand for the initial conditions that prevailed at the time of creation.

Where did this equation and its constants come from? Did it precede creation? Did it have a prior existence? Plato certainly thought so, as do some of the greatest living thinkers. If so, where did it exist? Are there other universes with different equations? Could an equation such as this possibly evolve from a process of trial and error? Is the idea that such an equation exists at all just an illusion? Are scientists chasing rainbows in trying to find it? Or is there a completely different paradigm they should be trying in order to model ultimate reality?

These are all serious questions that occupy the minds of some of the greatest living thinkers. There are many different opinions, but as of yet no convincing answers are available.

Purpose

Where are the laws of nature leading the Universe? Is it on a pre-planned course to somewhere, or is it being blown by some kind of celestial wind not knowing where exactly it will end up? Looking at its present status, one could say that one of its purposes is to create diversity – witness the diversity of the heavens, of the countless different habitats on earth and the diversity of the living world. This diversity may be an end in itself or could be just a stepping stone to somewhere else.

Is our universe like a falling stone, determinate, predictable, purposeful and structured? Or is like the weather – indeterminate, unpredictable, chaotic and approximate?

Whatever the answer, it is clear that imperfection plays a leading role. To achieve its ends, nature has taken the scenic route. From billions of possibly hostile universes it chose the one most supportive of the development of life. It ensured a lumpy start for the selected universe, creating imperfections which would in time clump together and form galaxies, stars and worlds. For at least one of these worlds, it created an extraordinary chain of coincidences to ensure a place where life could develop. Imperfection played many important roles along the way:

> A universe to sustain life may have been an exercise in probability.
>
> Right from creation, imperfection appeared and evoked a far-reaching response.
>
> Creation of our own improbable world was a result of chance and coincidences.
>
> Man's access to the secrets of nature is second-hand and imperfect.
>
> His laws of science are mimics of the real laws and subject to decay and death.
>
> Quantum mechanics and evolution are random and indeterminate.
>
> All the laws of nature need imbalances and imperfections to work on.

This is not the conventional view of creation. Einstein has said that God was infinitely more subtle than we give him credit for. Perhaps this is how this new scenario should be viewed.

Chapter 4.
THE LIVING WORLD

In the living world, we encounter many wonderful events. We see the astonishing metamorphosis of the humble caterpillar as a new butterfly emerges, unfolds its long legs and beautiful wings and flies away. We wonder how this miracle has come about and our thoughts may run as follows:

> *This is surely perfection in action. Anything that man can devise pales into insignificance compared to this. This must be the work of someone or something a million times more intelligent than we are.*

The truth is that imperfection lies behind this miracle. Life's path has been strewn with errors, accidents and mistakes. The fundamental processes of life are based on random mutations, duplications, omissions and errors. Disease, decay and death abound. Yet in the end beings of extraordinary beauty have emerged. How can this be?

Life began somewhere as a single cell. Where and how remains a mystery. It found a supportive home on our planet. Here it began to replicate itself to create millions of other cells. It learned how to customise itself in order to perform specialised functions like seeing and hearing; then how to assemble these functions into living creatures of ever-increasing complexity. It eventually produced specialised cells to make brains and support intelligence. It did all this by trial and error over billions of years

There were three major phases – preparation, emergence and propagation. A rough time-scale is instructive. (Times are given in millions of years ago - mya).

Time, mya	
Preparation	
13,700	The Big Bang – Creation of the Universe
8,800	Formation of Milky Way Galaxy
4,500	Formation of the earth
Emergence	
4,000	Emergence of primitive life
1,000	First multi-cellular life
Propagation	
400	Emergence of insects, fish, plants
200	First mammals, followed by birds
65	Dinosaurs die out
2.5	Primitive humans

All along the way imperfection has been ever-present.

What is Life?

There is no simple accepted definition of what life is. It is the characteristic that distinguishes plants and animals from inorganic matter. Biologists generally define seven characteristics which distinguish a living object from its inanimate components.

Organisation

All living things are made up of one or more cells. The cells are organised into complex structures, each cell performing a specific function such as brain and eye cells.

Regulation

There are regulation mechanisms to maintain a stable internal state such as a steady blood temperature. The organism can also rebuild and repair itself.

Growth

The organism can increase in size and complexity and can change its form and physiological makeup, e.g. the caterpillar to butterfly transformation.

Use of Energy

It can take in food from its environment and convert it into the energy needed for it to function and grow.

Sensitivity

It is aware of its surroundings being sensitive to light, sound, heat, gravity and pressure.

Adaptation

It is able to change in response to its environment. This ability is fundamental to its ability to evolve over time and thus survive.

Reproduction

It can produce offspring and pass its own hereditary information on to the new organism.

The Cell

Cells are the smallest living unit. Each living organism is constructed from one or more cells; all its vital functions occur within them. Cells can be specialised to do specific functions, such as making eyes or bones. Cells emerged about 4 billion years ago. They are visible only under the microscope. All cells come from pre-existing cells. Each contains the hereditary information necessary for regulating cell functions and for transmitting information to the next generation of cells. A cell is composed of various amino acids, arranged in a rather particular way.

As we get to know more about the functioning of the individual cell, the more we realise just how complex it is. Living matter is made up of the same basic elements as inanimate matter, except that it is organised differently. We are beginning to appreciate just how complex this organisation really is. Within the cell, thousands of small chemical interactions occur each minute. It resembles a busy factory, with thousands of operatives continually on the move doing their job – sensing, signalling, digesting, manufacturing, correcting, repairing, defending, replicating etc. The control center of the cell is contained within its *nucleus*.

The Secret of Life

One of the pivotal moments of the last century surely was when Crick and Watson[28] walked into their pub in Cambridge and shouted: *We have found the secret of Life.* They had discovered the double helix structure of the DNA molecule. In a simple elegant structure, DNA held all the information required to build a living organism, even a living person. The discovery triggered off massive research and has resulted in a revolution in biology and in our understanding of the mechanisms of life. Today we know:

---

[28]   James D **Watson** and Francis **Crick**, co-discoverers of the structure of DNA in 1953, Nobel Prize 1962

- The detailed biological mechanisms behind evolution
- Exactly how genetics and heredity works
- How to genetically engineer crops and animals
- How to trace the source of genetic disorders and perhaps cure them
- How to repair damaged organs by the use of stem-cell techniques

We have learned that no two people ever have been the same – we can prove it using the absolute uniqueness of their DNA. We can trace migrations of peoples over thousands of years by tracing flows of DNA across continents. The race to master, control and exploit one of nature's deepest secrets continues apace, and will dominate much of scientific effort for all of this century.

DNA

DNA is life's instruction manual. It contains all the instructions needed to create and maintain a living organism. These instructions have been arrived at over millions of years of trial and error and are now coded into its double helix.

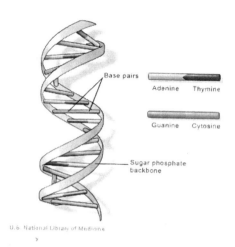

DNA takes the form of a double-wound helix.[29] It consists of a long chain of base pairs, each made up of 2 loosely connected nucleotides. The base pairs are like the steps of a stairs which are held together by a backbone which resembles the handrail of a spiral staircase. The two strands contain the same biological information, held in reverse order, and this information is duplicated when the two strands are separated for cell division or reproduction. The chain is somewhat fragile and can easily be broken, re-sequenced and reconnected. Similarly the two strands can be easily torn apart.

The base pairs are like the letters of the alphabet. They are organised into sentences (genes) which in turn are organised into chapters (chromosomes). The sentence or gene is the unit of instruction. In the human instruction manual, there are 23 chapters, 25,000 sentences and 3,000,000,000 letters. The sequence of the instructions is all important. A change in sequence conveys a very different message, similar to changing the sequence of letters within a word. Every single person and living organism has a different DNA. Such a degree of variation is possible as there is nearly an infinite number of ways in which 3 billion base pairs can be assembled and sequenced.

---

[29]   The DNA Helix Image courtesy the US National Library of Medicine. ghr.nlm. nih.gov

An organism's complete set of DNA, including all its genes, is called its genome. In humans a copy of the genome is contained within each cell. The Human Genome Project is an ambitious international effort to identify the sequence of the human genome, and identify the location and functions of all the genes it contains. Once completed, it will have mapped out the complex blueprint of life.

Control System

To maintain everything work in synch, a sophisticated control system is needed. This consists of DNA and RNA located in the nucleus of the cell. DNA contains all the instructions needed to create and maintain a living organism. The instructions are held in coded form.

The RNA molecule reads and interprets the instructions just as we interpret instructions written in a book. It conveys these instructions to the parts of the cell that create proteins, form new cells, replace and repair damaged cells and perform a host of other complex functions.

How did RNA learn how to do all these things? Is it somehow pre-programmed with some sophisticated software? Or is it reading some *How-To* manual written in the skies? We simply do not know. One day we will be able to account for the origin of all the components of the cell and their special arrangement, but the origins of the intelligence that transforms these into a living entity remains a mystery.

Bill Gates[30] has remarked: *Human DNA is like a computer program, but is far, far more complex than anything we have devised so far.*

> A skilled engineer, armed with a box of components and same simple tools, can build a small computer. When finished, he has simply a set of re-arranged components. The computer does not come to life until he loads the operating system into its memory bank. This is the system software, which tells each component what to do, and when and how to do it. With it, the computer is now *alive* and can perform an array of intelligent functions, such as computation and image processing.
>
> The analogy holds true for the cell. The origin of its physical components and their arrangement can in time be fully explained, but the origin of its intelligence is a deeper issue.

Preparation for Life

Preparation (8,800 mya to 4500 mya)

Our earth was formed as a suitable home for life through an extraordinary set of co-incidences. These co-incidences have all the appearance of randomness, driven by imbalances in the distribution of matter and energy across our solar system. These imbalances can be traced back to the creation of our universe, the selection of its initial startup parameters and the early lumpiness of the infant universe. After this, the laws of physics and chemistry took over to create millions of different habitats.

---

[30]   Bill **Gates**, b.1955 Seattle, co-founder of Microsoft, the world's largest software business. *The Road Ahead*, 1996

The Raw Materials

Earth, for millions of years, possessed all the materials necessary for supporting life:

Oxygen, Nitrogen

> The principal constituents of air

Hydrogen

> With oxygen, the principle constituent of water
>
> Free hydrogen may have been available in early volcanoes

Carbon

> Carbon was made available by the volatile nature of the earth in the beginning, where volcanoes spewed various elements into the earth's atmosphere.

Ammonia, methane

> These are rich sources of nitrogen and hydrogen, and were readily available through early volcanic activity.

Amino acids are the building blocks of proteins, which in turn are the building blocks of life. Amino-acids are complex molecules composed of oxygen, hydrogen, carbon and nitrogen. There are 20 standard amino acids involved in the life process. Nine standard amino acids are called *essential* for humans because they cannot be created from other compounds by the human body, and so must be taken in as food.

It is not clear how the first amino acids came to be synthesized from simple organic compounds. Scientists are agreed that some very special environment was needed in the early universe, an environment that no longer exists and which is very difficult to replicate in a laboratory. Views differ as to where this special environment may have occurred, some suggestions being:

In volcanic clouds laden with methane, ammonia and nitrogen and subject to lightening

In some kind of primordial soup, rich in chemicals

In deep sea vents, rich in chemical and thermal energy

In certain mineral clays known to arrange themselves into organised patterns

Under deep icecaps which would have protected early fragile organic compounds

On some sea shore under the influence of radio-activity

Emergence

Creation (about 4000 mya)

Relatively soon after the earth was formed, life appeared. While time estimates differ, the *eagerness* of life to exist was apparent from the beginning. A contributing factor was the special nature of our ecosphere, the area of the planet capable of sustaining life. The theory of evolution does not attempt to explain how life began on earth – only how it evolved afterwards. Much research continues into the very origins of life. Scientists can even begin to think of one day creating life from scratch in one of our laboratories, perhaps creating some very simple bacteria. Of unique interest is how human intelligence and intellect slowly emerged from very basic life forms into miracles of cellular organization.

Creation of the first living cell was a momentous event. At that moment, the parameters that define a living thing were determined.

The internal organization of the cell was put in place. A form of lumpiness was built in, in the form of uneven mutations. A response to these mutations came from the environment, and the laws of natural selection and organic chemistry took over.

The First Cell

The living cell is something of extraordinary complexity. All are agreed that some extraordinary set of events and initial conditions was needed to make it happen. There are many theories as to how the first cell emerged. Research is focused on a number of areas:

Availability of the raw materials necessary for building the first cell.

How the first complex organic compounds could have evolved

The simplest possible organisms that could have started the cycle of life

The possibility of self-organisation of complex molecules

Whether life could have started elsewhere in space and been transported here

How the sophisticated control mechanisms of the cell could have emerged

All attempts by the finest laboratories of the world have failed so far failed to produce one living cell from scratch, even given the explosion of knowledge of the last few years.

Some scientists take a top-down approach, and are trying to determine whether there may have been extremely simple forms of life that no longer exist and which may have acted as stepping stones towards more complex subsequent forms. Single-cell bacteria are the smallest known living things, and scientists can now strip them down to their most basic form, while still retaining the characteristics of life. Some complex amino acid molecules show some of the characteristics of life, being able to divide and reproduce. As we study ever smaller forms of life, such as single-cell viruses, the border line between life and non-life gets narrower, but we seem nowhere close to making a leap across the great divide.

There are many systems that appear to organise themselves without the intervention of any external agency. They are found in physics, chemistry, biology, and economics and in human cultures. Simple examples are colonies of bees and the flocking behaviour of birds. From simple components, they can build quite complex structures. Chemists have been able to observe many examples of self-organizing behaviour with simple molecules, but are not able to explain the complex self-assembly process needed to create biomolecules.

Perhaps life did not begin on earth at all, but was brought here from elsewhere in space, a notion known as panspermia. Dr. Carl Pilcher[31] of NASA has commented *that the discovery of glycine in a comet supports the idea that the fundamental building blocks of life are prevalent in space, and strengthens the argument that life in the universe may be common rather than rare.* However, even if this turns out to be true, a new question arises as to how life began elsewhere in space.

---

[31]   Dr Carl **Pilcher,** Director, NASA Astrobiology Institute since 2006

Propagation

Propagation (1000 mya to the present)

Once created, life propagated itself with an astonishing virtuosity. It was driven by inbuilt flaws in the genetic process and the response of the environment to these flaws. Genetic mutation and natural selection started off the processes which eventually yielded the astonishing diversity and virtuosity of the natural world.

Disturbances

In spite of the sophisticated control system in the cell, mistakes occur. Many of these occur in the course of cell division and replication.

Cell division occurs while creating egg and sperm cells during sexual reproduction. The sequence of the base pairs in the egg, the sperm, the new helix and even in the young embryo can be altered by omissions, insertions, duplications and re-sorting. The process has often been likened to the shuffling of two decks of cards. The errors are many but usually small. Large errors could result in the loss of vital information necessary for the survival of the organism.

Cell replication is the process of creating new body cells for growth and replacement. A cell duplicates all of its contents, including its DNA, and splits to form two identical cells. Errors can be caused by environmental factors such as ultraviolet radiation from the sun, or can occur by mistakes in the copying process itself. Some, but not all, of these changes can be passed on to the offspring.

The consequences of the mistakes may be positive or negative. On the positive side, new traits can appear which enhance the ability of the organism to survive and multiply in a given environment. The negative consequences may include death of the organism, genetic diseases such as Down's syndrome, inability to procreate, and unwanted traits.

Mutation is a permanent change in the DNA sequence that makes up a gene. It alters the genetic messages passed on to subsequent generations. Drawing an analogy with the early physical universe, one could say that the early living world very quickly became *lumpy*. There was unevenness, imbalances and local perturbations.

Natural Selection

Nature's response to mutation was natural selection. The process was first described by Darwin[32], having observed various mutations on his travels to the Galapagos Islands. There he observed a group of about 15 species of finch (since known as Darwin's Finches). All were unique to the islands. They were of different sizes, and Darwin noticed important differences in the shape and size of their beaks. He surmised that the beaks had become highly adapted to the different food sources available on the different islands. He wrote in 1845: *Seeing this gradation and diversity of structure in one small, intimately connected group of birds, one might really fancy that from an original paucity of birds on this archipelago, one species had been taken and modified for different ends.*

He deduced that mutation can give an individual a reproductive advantage over others (such as a beak better adapted to local food

---

[32]   Charles Robert **Darwin** FRS, 1809–1882. English naturalist, inventor of the Theory of Evolution

sources).This advantage will be passed on from parent to child. Even if the reproductive advantage is very slight, over many generations any heritable advantage will become dominant in the population. In this way the natural environment of an organism selects traits that confer a reproductive advantage, causing gradual changes or evolution of life. Thus was born the Theory of Evolution.

Other Perturbations

Evolution does not explain all the changes observed in population characteristics. Other random factors, such as gene flow and genetic drift, also play a significant role.

Gene flow is the exchange of genes between populations and between species. It can be caused by the movement of individuals between separate populations of organisms, as might be caused by travel and migration. It can therefore be a source of variation that is new to a population or to a species.

Genetic drift occurs when population changes occur by chance events, not at all related to evolution. A given characteristic, such as red hair, can be lost forever just because of statistical randomness. The effect is more easily observed in small populations rather than large ones. Natural disasters can play a part. A random event, like a volcanic eruption, may kill a large portion of a population and the survivors may have a quite different mix of characteristics from the previous population.

Population Genetics

This is the branch of science that deals with the statistical analysis of the inheritance and prevalence of genes in populations. It is essentially the application of statistical methods to the genetics of populations. It provides a theoretical basis for processes such as natural selection, genetic drift, mutation and gene flow. It studies the forces that may alter the genetic composition of a population over time, such as recurrent mutation, migration, intermixture between groups, differential fertility rates, and the random changes in cell reproduction. The principles of population genetics may be applied to plants and animals as well as humans.

Human Intervention

The process of evolution eventually brought man onto the scene. This new arrival was able to observe the way that life processes operated under nature, but was not satisfied with these. He wanted to speed them up and bend them to suit better his own particular needs. Using his intelligence and intellect, he quickly learned how to gain control of the genetic process. By plant breeding, he could change the frequency with which a specific trait occurs in a population. More recently, he can directly change the sequence of the genetic code and thus intervene in the life process at its most fundamental level.

Plant Breeding

This has been practiced for thousands of years. Initially it consisted of selecting and breeding plants with desired characteristics, and discarding those which did not. Desired characteristics might be taste, appearance, food value, size of yield, resistance to pests, or suitability to climate. Hybridization aims, via cross-pollination, to combine together into one plant desired traits found in different plants.

Genetic Engineering

This is the direct manipulation of the genes of an organism. It involves the transfer of genes between organisms or changes in the sequence of a gene. It has the same objectives as plant breeding but provides accelerated results. The resulting organism is then said to be genetically modified (GM). For example, crop plants can be given a gene from an arctic fish, so they produce an antifreeze protein in their leaves. This can help prevent frost damage. Other genes that can be put into crops include a natural insecticide taken from bacteria. The insecticide kills insects that eat the plants, but is harmless to people.

GM foods are now commonplace. They raise many concerns, as people fear that the modified genes may escape into wild life with unpredictable consequences. Also that they tend to pass some control of agriculture from the traditional farmer to large commercial corporations which have advanced laboratories at their disposal.

Gene Therapy.

The kind of technology used in genetic engineering is also being developed to treat people with genetic disorders. Gene therapy works by trying to replace the gene that causes a disease with a gene that will work properly. The new gene is put in after the person has grown up and become ill, so any new gene will not be inherited by the children. Again this kind of interference with the life process at its most fundamental level raises many fears, and serious opposition exists in many quarters.

Role of Imperfection

Imperfection played an important role in all phases of life development.

In the *preparation for life*, over billions of years it spawned a myriad of components and habitats, until eventually a very unique combination was reached.

As to the *creation of life*, there is still no explanation as to how and where this happened, but it could not have occurred without the years of preparation. It represented a major *transition*. From it, a new kingdom was born - the kingdom of life, which blossomed and soon covered all the earth. Emergence of life is one of a number of transitions that have taken place and which appear to share common characteristics. These will be examined in the context of a new theory to be presented in Chapter 10.

The *propagation of life* has depended on flaws, mutations and sheer chance. Without these flaws, new-born life would have stalled in its original form.

Checkpoint

When man finally arrived on the scene, everything changed. Here was a being able to observe, reflect and be self-aware. Yet flawed in many ways, and capable of destroying the very nature from which it emerged in the first place.

Chapter 5.
THE WORLD OF MAN

Nature created man with many imperfections. Physically he is comparatively weak. Mentally he is limited in many ways. Behaviourally he is distinctly fallible. Fortunately nature also provided man with the means to counteract these flaws – it bestowed on him intelligence and intellect. With these he was able to initiate responses to each inadequacy. To compensate for his physical limitations he invented artefacts such as tools, weapons, cars and aeroplanes. To compensate for his mental limitations he invented calculators, computers and the internet. To constrain his behavioural deficiencies he devised many complex restraining systems such as laws, customs and religions.

Physical –The Response

Nature from the beginning imposed on man many severe physical limitations. He walks and runs slowly. He cannot fly and swims poorly. He has a comparatively narrow range of vision, hearing and smell. He is no match for the large predators. Exposed, he suffers seriously from extremes of weather. These seem poor enough specifications for a master of the world.

However when intelligence and inventiveness arrived on the scene, things began to change. Inventiveness brought tools and artefacts. The earliest artefacts were rudimentary tools made of flint stone, often interpreted as the first signs of the emergence of *Homo Sapiens*[33]. Man learned quickly how to harness the forces of nature to his own advantage. Nature's energy such as wind, water and fire could be harnessed to do work. Its vast store of materials could be moulded and shaped to make things. It just required a leap of imagination to see the possibilities.

Slowly an answer was found to most physical limitations. An astonishing array of devices was devised to assist in every conceivable task. Thousands of new artefacts appeared as invention began to transform lives. A popular entertainment on television is to nominate the ten greatest inventions of all time. The ten below are a typical sample of those chosen.

The Automobile	The Use of Electricity
The Steam Engine	The Printing Press
The Aeroplane	The Computer
The Pill	The FlushingToilet
Penicillin	The Internet

These inventions were originally intended to help individuals, but it rapidly became clear that they were also engines of social revolution. The automobile has had a huge impact on how whole communities live, work, shop and socialise. The Pill has launched a revolution in sexual behaviour. The flushing toilet is included, not for its technical

---

[33] Homo Sapiens, "wise man", the human species, emerged about 200,000 years ago

sophistication, but because, without it, modern towns and cities would have been impossible.

> *I believe that there never was a creator of a philosophical system who did not confess at the end of his life that he had wasted his time. It must be admitted that the inventors of the mechanical arts have been much more useful to men that the inventors of syllogisms. He who imagined a ship towers considerably above him who imagined innate ideas.*
>
> --Voltaire [34]

The invention of the engine has been one of the significant landmarks in human history. A recent exhibition in Munich[35] traced the development of engines and the consequences that followed them. Below are listed some of the types of engines and the revolutions they gave rise to.

The waterwheel	Powered the first mills to grind the corn and make flour.
The steam engine	Powered the first factories, ships and railways.
The petrol engine	Made possible the modern car.
The electric motor	Found in our hair dryers, vacuum cleaners, even toothbrushes.
The diesel engine	Drives huge ships, tractors, trucks and bulldozers.
The jet engine	Has reduced our globe to a few hours flight.

---

[34] **Voltaire.,** Francois-Marie Arouet, 1694-1778, Paris. French writer and philosopher

[35] Deutsches Museum, Munich / Energietechnik

| The rocket engine | Brought the first man to the moon. |
| The solar engine | Will probably take man to distant planets and galaxies. |

The Price

Underlying many of the main technological advances is the concept of nature as an exploitable resource. Man could turn nature on itself, calling on its resources to counteract the limitations that nature had imposed on him in the first place.

Nature has its weak points if only you can find them - James Watt[36]

The more that technology advances, the greater becomes its demand for resources. Many benefits accrue, but they come at a price. Nature's resources are not limitless; its ability to recover from man's demands is not infinite. Its age-old balances can be upset, and changes to this balance could become irreversible. Many begin to see ominous warning signs all around us. The hazards foreseen are:

Global warming with catastrophic changes to weather patterns

Destruction of the ozone layer

Pollution of the oceans with the loss of marine life

Destruction of valued habitats for animals such as the rain forests

Loss of biodiversity, the source of many of our foods and medicines

Risk of nuclear accidents and nuclear war

---

[36] James **Watt**, 1736-1819. Scottish inventor and engineer, Developer of the steam engine.

Carl Sagan[37] wrote that all high technology civilisations tend to self-destruct; that their demands on resources eventually destroy the very environment that supports them. We may have already taken the first steps on such a path.

A Fable

There was a large fishbowl with many fish. At its base were many succulent cacti like plants which provided ample food for all the fish. The fish could not see outside the fishbowl as it was made of one-way glass, one could see in but not out. There was a tiny hole at the top through which shone a thin pencil of blue light. One day a fish was born with super-intelligence. It resented the fishbowl because it was dark and cold. It found that by eating more and more it could swim faster and longer than all the other fish. To safeguard its food supply it started to build a fence around the food source, a fence made up of many spikes taken from the cacti. It became undisputed master of the fishbowl.

The fish grew smarter and smarter and developed extraordinary qualities such as invention, creativity and genius. It began to think of what lay outside the fishbowl and wondered at the pencil of light coming through the tiny hole. This stirred something within it. It began to dream of escaping the fishbowl and its oppressive constraints, into the blue light above, inventing many scenarios to this effect.

All worked very well except that the cacti started to wilt. They too needed their spikes for protection, but were now stripped.

---

[37]   Dr. Carl Edward **Sagan**, 1934-1996, American astronomer and futurologist. *Cosmos, 1980.*

Suddenly one morning the smart fish awoke to find that the cacti had all died.

Mental – The Response

In the mental world, the microchip is the equivalent of the engine. It consists of a set of electronic components such as transistors and sensors mounted on a small plate of silicon. Millions of components can be mounted on a tiny plate. The sensors make the chip responsive to the world around it and the transistors can provide any kind of logical response required. Microchips supply the intelligence for thousands of machines and gadgets that we use on an everyday basis. If the engine does the physical work for us, the microchip does the thinking work for us.

To help with complex calculations, the first solution was the calculator; first mechanical, then electronic. Later came the computer. The modern computer can carry out computations at unimaginable speeds and can store vast amounts of information accurately and speedily. In some facets, its power far exceeds that of the human brain.

Our present world has an insatiable thirst for new electronic devices such as smartphones, calculators, and computers. The pressure for new inventions is intense. Smartphones and social networks are moving beyond being just artefacts; they are becoming almost an essential part of the personality of the owner. As we move forward, the border lines between the person and the artefact will become still more blurred. We are beginning to see microchips embedded into the human body in the form of pacemakers, brain-controlled artificial limbs, etc. The future will see much more of this integration.

In the hands of a modern scientist, the real world consists of a set of abstract mathematical equations running within the memory of some very powerful computer. To him, the computer and its models are the ultimate reality. The computer can, for example, handle models of the entire universe with four or ten dimensions, but our minds are grounded in three dimensions and find difficulty in envisaging anything else.

The computer made possible the internet. First designed to share information within a university, it has developed with astonishing speed in many unforeseen directions. Its ability to provide instant access to information, stored perhaps thousands of miles away, lead many to claim that all human knowledge will soon become available through it at the touch of a button. Its worldwide network not alone provides information access, but also carries television, telephone, video conferencing and social networks. It can now be said to connect the world. On the Facebook social network, there are more than one billion members, able to communicate almost instantly with each other. The social consequences of this are far-reaching.

The internet is a good example of a self-organising system. Nobody is in charge of it. There is no master plan. Nobody knows where it will go next, just as nobody could have predicted where it is now. Yet it grows with astonishing speed, grows daily in complexity and gives the appearance of knowing where it is going.

Like the engine, the microchip has revolutionised our lives. It has helped us individually to carry our many complex mental tasks, but in the wider context it has had significant social consequences.

Behavioural – The Response

Few will disagree with the thesis that behaviourally man is a flawed creature. A reading of the newspaper provides us with a daily chronicle. There are shocking wars in many parts of the world, resulting in untold human misery and death. Bitter ethnic and religious conflicts abound. Murders are commonplace and still make the headlines. We read of jail sentences imposed for a myriad of transgressions. We see pictures illustrating the massive inequalities that exist in various societies. We find it hard to find some good news. There is much more imperfection that perfection to be found. In an attempt to constrain this flawed behaviour, it has been necessary to design a myriad of social, legal and religious systems. These are mostly based on the idea of punishment. Sanctions of various types are designed to act as deterrents to the transgressors. A few promise rewards for good behaviour instead of sanctions for bad behaviour.

Etiquette

An extensive etiquette has built up surrounding the drinking of tea. Many different sets of rituals have evolved in various parts of the world; a book could be filled with the details. The rules cover how to make tea, pour it, and how to correctly use the spoon to stir it. The rules also outline the manner in which the social status of each of the participants must be observed.

Social life is made up of thousands of such conventions. We begin to teach these conventions to babies of less than one year old. As infants we learn the maxims - *don't do this, don't do that* - and they remain with us throughout our life. Many of the rules of society are unwritten but all are well aware of them. Their purpose is to maintain order in society and to prevent behaviour that may be offensive to others. Most rules have had a practical origin, but many have outlived their origins and have become meaningless conventions.

Legal Systems

Each country has its own law library, containing all the statutes and laws that apply within its territory. These statutes have been built up over centuries. Political leaders have spent many countless hours devising them. Prisons are full of people who have dared to transgress them. Most legal systems are essentially punishment-based, and many people argue against their effectiveness in preventing crime. In the past, punishments were much more horrible than they are now and they still did not eradicate crime. However effective alternatives to punishment appear to be either not practicable or not put into effect.

Much of our society seems to be controlled by lawyers, judges and advocates. Many governments are beholden to their authority. Judges are deemed to be above politics and have the power at times to dismiss a government. At international level, we see the development of courts with wide powers to try and condemn political leaders suspected of genocide, war crimes and crimes against humanity. We cannot contemplate any kind of peaceful future without this extensive array of constraining institutions.

Guidelines of Religion

The Old Testament relates how God gave Moses the Ten Commandments, written on tablets of stone on the top of Mount Sinai. These commandments still form the basis for the moral teaching of all the Christian and Jewish churches. Different groups follow slightly different traditions for interpreting and numbering them. Below is the Catholic version.

The Ten Commandments

1. I am the Lord your God. You shall not have strange Gods before me.
2. You shall not take the name of the Lord your God in vain
3. Remember to keep holy the Lord's Day
4   Honour your father and your mother
5   You shall not kill
6. You shall not commit adultery
7. You shall not steal
8. You shall not bear false witness against your neighbour
9. You shall not covet your neighbour's wife
10. You shall not covet your neighbour's goods

The first three commandments deal with man's relationship with God. The remaining seven deal with his inherent tendency to theft, dishonesty, murder and adultery. The exhortations are mostly negative in nature but can be restated in positive form as:

Love God. Love your neighbour

Different religions have their own sets of commandments, usually set out in the Holy Books of each religion. All have the same objective of helping people to lead *good lives*. Billions of people worldwide try to live good lives by faithfully following the tenets of their own religion.

Where did all the human frailties come from? Evolutionists say they are a throwback to our animal origins where aggressiveness, possessiveness and sexual opportunism were essential elements for survival. Some religions teach that God created man perfect in his own likeness, but that he fell from grace by acts of his own free will.

Goodness

Alongside man's many frailties, there exists also an innate sense of goodness. This in the longer term always seems to prevail. There exists much evil, but in the end it is always defeated by the forces of good. *Good triumphs in the end* is a positive message to those who fear that the forces of evil cannot be defeated.

> The *wheels of God grind slowly, but they grind*
> *surely.* - An old Irish proverb

One can ask: *Where did goodness come from?* Some religions teach that it is a direct gift from God to man at birth. Plato proposed that man is born with an inherited sense of the virtues that make up goodness – justice, truth, kindness and a sense of morality. Evolutionists have much difficulty in fitting goodness into a theory based on the survival of the fittest. Nevertheless they assert that some aspects, such as altruism, can be explained within evolution theory. Whatever its origin, goodness remains a powerful force in enabling man to come to terms with his many imperfections.

This is the very perfection of a man, to find out his own imperfections.

- St Augustine[38]

Society

The concept of *human society* has arisen frequently in the above discussion. It covers the entire spectrum of social relations between humans.

The responses to man's frailties have led indirectly to the creation of ever more sophisticated forms of society. The level of social relations between humans has increased enormously as a result of easier travel, television, phones, internet and social networks. A global culture is emerging and shared institutions now include such things as pop music, cinema, Google, Facebook and Twitter. We can see a form of evolution taking place. At the level of primitive life, the individual cell learned how to specialise and combine with other cells in order to create organisms of real complexity. Perhaps we are seeing the same process occurring with human beings. Individuals are becoming part of shared networks of ever widening power and complexity. All will soon be working off the same information base. It is interesting to speculate what the end point of this evolutionary process might be and what kind of human domain might eventually emerge.

Much of what is described above can be represented as responses to man's flawed nature. The responses are initiated by society, as it attempts to legislate for the common good, often at the expense

---

[38] **Augustine** of Hippo (Roman Africa, now Algeria). Latin philosopher and theologian, 354-430. His writings were very influential in the development of western Christianity

of the individual. A big slice of human activity has been devoted to finding suitable responses.

One can envisage a huge *system manual* that records all the categories of response that have emerged to date. Its chapters include the rules of good social behaviour, the law libraries of the world and the teachings of the religions. This system manual is being expanded by the day as new technical concepts emerge and new behavioural constraints prove necessary. Man's imperfections remain largely unchanged, but subject to a multitude of constraints. These constraints allow human society to function smoothly and maintain a balance between the rights of the individual and the good of society.

Chapter 6.
CONSCIOUSNESS ARRIVES

Michelangelo's paintings in the Sistine Chapel in Rome represent perhaps the pinnacle of medieval art. They consist of 33 panels depicting scenes from the Old Testament and the Gospels, covering the entire walls and ceiling. It took Michelangelo ten years to complete the work. The scale and beauty of his concepts leave one dumbfounded. It is hard to conceive of anything more magnificent. One is tempted to use the word perfection.

The paintings bring us deep into the mental model that Michelangelo and his contempories had of his universe - the basic questions of God, man, creation, judgment, good and evil. Since early times man has been creating such models. The cave drawings at Lascaux in France, dating from around 15,000BC were among the first models of animals and man's relationship with them. Later models were couched in the languages such as science and philosophy.

These models are essential for the conscious mind. They help it to come to terms with its capricious and often perplexing dwelling place. It has a deep need to understand its surroundings, formalise them as rule sets, represent them in abstract models, and thereby feel better prepared to meet their challenges. From this need there grew a great forest. It was populated by ideas and concepts and with art, science, mathematics, philosophy and religions. Vast libraries were needed to house the resulting *conceptual repertoire.*

This is consciousness in action. One may ask: What is it? Where did it come from? Is it perfection or imperfection driven?

Intelligence

Early forms of life began to develop a central nervous system. Together with the development of sensory organs, they began to become aware of their environment. They could sense where food was and seek it out. They could migrate to a warmer climate when the weather got cold. They could sense the presence of an enemy and take evasive action. Even a jellyfish, with an extremely primitive nervous system, can sense its environment and move to a more favourable place. This has been sufficient to enable it to survive almost unchanged for millions of years.

As central nervous systems became more and more sophisticated, a new phenomenon appeared – intelligence. Conferring an enormous survival advantage, intelligence levels grew rapidly. Animals, such as the lion, learned how to live in communities and develop rules of social co-existence. They could take control of a territory and defend it against all-comers.

Eventually a being emerged that learned how to use tools. With this one step, it came to dominate its environment and compensate for its ever-present hazards. It built houses to shut out the weather, and knew how to write books to pass its knowledge on to its young. It learned how to harness the resources of nature for its own benefit. It eventually could build spaceships.

The transition occurred about 200,000 years ago. Intelligence turned into consciousness. Homo Sapiens had arrived. Human beings became aware of their own thinking, of themselves as beings and of their strange environment. They could mentally stand outside the fragile body in which their consciousness was housed and outside the hostile environment in which this body was constrained to live. They began to ask questions. They needed to know why everything was the way it was, and why they were there in the middle of it all.

What is consciousness?

Most people have a general idea of what consciousness is, but it is very difficult to define it precisely. A definition such as *the fact of awareness by the mind of itself and the world* does not help much, as the word *awareness* in turn requires definition and is frequently reverse-defined in terms of consciousness. Other words associated with consciousness are:

> Understanding, Awareness, Insight, Wisdom, Judgment, Inspiration, Imagination, Vision

Closely associated with consciousness is the concept of intellect. This has been defined as:

> The ability to learn, reason and think abstractly
> The capacity for understanding and knowledge

With this powerful mental toolkit, man was now in possession of a very powerful engine. The ability to model the future and to predict and plan would have conferred an enormous survival advantage.

There are many intelligent animals, such as the dog and the dolphin, but they do not display consciousness in the sense that they can say: *I exist* or ask: *Who am I?* It was once thought that consciousness was a function of brain size, but there are animals which have larger brains than man and do not have it. Modern computers have processing powers far ahead of the human brain, but we do not expect them to exhibit any of the characteristics of consciousness

Theologians contend that consciousness is a function of the human soul. They teach that each of us is endowed with a living soul at birth, something separate from the body and the mind. At death, the soul lives on and carries our consciousness with it. The higher functions such as art, imagination and spirituality are products of the soul rather of than the mechanical and electrical processes of the body. Billions of people intuitively accept this solution to the mystery of consciousness.

At scientific level, a lot of advanced research is currently being done by neurologists into what is called the Global Workspace Theory. This runs as follows:

> The brain consists of a large number of neural networks which are in constant activity, carrying out various information processing tasks such as interpreting the sounds that come from the ears. Their internal activities are the subconscious. The brain is equipped with a global workspace, which resembles the transient memory of

a computer. This workspace can run only one dominant activity at a time. It is consciousness that decides what that activity is. The resulting serial activity constitutes our stream of consciousness. The content of the global workspace is known to all the individual networks, who now order their activity to best provide it with the necessary inputs. The global workspace may be a special network of neurons distributed right across the brain, it may be an electromagnetic field, or it might be something much more mysterious. Its seat has not yet been located.

The process of thought implies a control system, along the lines of what was discussed earlier at cell level. Neurologists are making significant strides in identifying the different components of the brain, but it takes an operating system to tell each component what to do and when and how to do it. The operating system of the brain is infinitely more complex than that of the living cell. It is it that guides and synchronises all our mental activities, and provides judgment and imagination and all the other components of consciousness. When Beethoven wrote the Ninth Symphony, no doubt millions of firing neurons were involved. But a miracle of synchronisation was needed to produce the desired result. We have no idea where the mind's operating system came from. The physical components it uses may have arisen through evolutionary forces, but the control system itself is of a totally different order.

Human consciousness is just about the last surviving mystery. A mystery is a phenomenon that people don't know how to think about - yet. There have been other great mysteries: the mystery of the origin of the universe, the mystery of life and reproduction, and the mystery of the design to be found in nature, the mysteries of time, space, and gravity. These were not just areas of scientific ignorance, but of utter bafflement and wonder. We do not yet have all the answers to any of the questions of cosmology and particle physics, molecular genetics and evolutionary theory, but we do know how to think about them. With consciousness, however, we are still in a terrible muddle. Consciousness stands alone today as a topic that often leaves even the most sophisticated thinkers tongue-tied and confused. And, as with all of the earlier mysteries, there are many who insist -- and hope -- that there will never be a demystification of consciousness.

- Daniel C Dennett[39]

Properly speaking, the unconscious is the real psychic; its inner nature is just as unknown to us as the reality of the external world, and it is just as imperfectly reported to us through the data of consciousness as is the external world through the indications of our sensory organs.

— Freud[40]

Responses

The emergence of consciousness created a whole new dynamic. It changed fundamentally the relationship between man and his environment. Man could now take control of the environment instead of being driven by it. Initially things changed very slowly, but, once

---

[39] Daniel C. **Dennett**, b.1942. American philosopher writer. *Consciousness Explained* 1991.

[40] Sigmund **Freud**, 1856-1939, Austrian neurologist and father of psychoanalysis, *The Interpretation of Dreams* Freud

started, the rate of change accelerated and in the end proved unstoppable.

Any living organism has a complex relationship with the environment in which it is constrained to live. Firstly it depends entirely on this environment for its very existence - its food, shelter, light, and heat. In return, this environment imposes many constraints on it, some of which can be quite irksome, even deadly – famine, disease, danger, decay and death. For millions of years, living things did not question the environment in which they lived. Plants grew wherever the wind blew their seed, and accepted whatever nutrients that nature brought their way. They had no choice or influence. They waited for food, heat, air and water to arrive to them. To survive, they had to continually adapt to whatever environment they found themselves in. Animals could choose their environment through movement and migration, and could protect a prized environment fiercely. They became adept at protecting themselves and their young against the hazards of nature. But they too had to adapt to survive. The environment was still in control.

Then Homo Sapiens arrived. Like all other living things, he observed the sun rise every morning. He too enjoyed its welcome rays, but he wanted to go further. He wanted to know *why* the sun rose like this every morning. He was not content until he found an answer that satisfied him.

Man's responses to his environment have gone through a number of distinct phases.

Understand

Man begins to observe his world with his new found toolkit. He starts to suspect that this world was created by another intelligence, one superior to his own, one who ordained the stars in the sky and also one who sent the violent storms and volcanic eruptions which threatened his very existence. He needed to understand the purpose and design hidden behind all this.

Model

Man begins to create in his head abstract models of what he sees around him. He begins to paint animals on his cave wall. As he advances, he learns how to create mathematical equations of the whole solar system and predict with precision how every heavenly body moves.

Master

Man begins to master his environment through agriculture, tools and knowledge. With his intellectual power, he reverses the direction of adaptation. He makes the environment adapt to him. Early man was at the mercy of his environment. Now the environment is at the mercy of man. He utilises its resources for his own benefit and has the ability to destroy it completely.

Exploit

Nature is considered as a gift to man, to be owned and enjoyed for his own exclusive benefit. Its resources become commodities, to be exploited as rapidly as possible. Little thought is given to whether the environment can indefinitely sustain this plunder. Engineering is often defined as *the harnessing of the resources of nature for the benefit of mankind.* Engineering flourishes.

Interpret

As a conscious being, man stands back and begins to interpret his own relationship with his environment. He reflects on his own internal responses to nature - physical, emotional and spiritual - and expresses these through the medium of art, debate, philosophy, and religion.

Realign

As man sees the damage he can inflict on his environment, he sees the need to realign his own behaviour towards it. He sees the need to change his responses to accommodate and protect the environment. Physical, mental, and emotional adjustments are required.

Escape

The ultimate desire is to be free of the environment altogether, to escape its dangers, constraints and limitations, and ultimately death. The ideal is a disembodied intelligence and consciousness free from all physical constraints.

Various combinations of these responses can be identified behind most of man's greatest intellectual pursuits. The responses may be disguised as art or science, but at base they all are different expressions of the seven phases of response outlined above.

The intellect finds itself in a strange dwelling place. It is housed in an imperfect host, the human body. It lives in an imperfect environment from which it cannot escape and its knowledge of which is limited to the sensory inputs available to it. Yet it is able to think outside this box. It is like a prisoner in a confined cell whose mind can travel thousands of miles in a fraction of a second but whose body remains rooted in one place. It feels that it really does not belong in this place and its ultimate desire is to escape. Thus begins the invention of myriads of different scenarios.

Abstraction

The greatest innovation of the intellect was its power of abstract thinking. Abstract thinking gave the ability to observe the world, to make mental models of it, and then manipulate these models independently of the original observation. Man developed a powerful set of mental tools to help in this manipulation.

An architect builds scale models of the building he is designing. These help him to visualise the future building in three dimensions. He can make changes in a few minutes that might take months in reality. His model is portable and can be put it on view in many different places. A mental model is much faster and even more flexible. It can manipulate concepts at high speed through logic, research, mathematics, engineering and debate. Herein lays its power.

Mathematicians call this process a domain change. We observe reality, the original domain, and transform this into the abstract world, a new domain. We manipulate the abstract model in the new domain and then apply the results back onto the original domain. We start imposing our mental models back onto the observed world. We are happy when nature starts to conform to our own internal abstract models.

A curious feature of our abstractions is that they appear perfect to us. The Plato triangle encountered earlier serves as a model. The image of the triangle we hold in our heads appears to us perfect, without flaws. The image is created by the mind to satisfy the mind, and it is the mind that adjudicates on its validity. Inside this closed world, there is no possibility of mismatch.

There is a mismatch however between the seemingly perfect images in our heads and the flawed world outside. We have constantly to readjust our internal images to try and reduce these mismatches. It is this tension, between the perfect and the imperfect that engages the intellect. It has to constantly reconcile its own imaginings of perfection with the flawed reality that the senses present to it.

As nature drifts towards disorder, our mental world goes in the other direction, trying to impose intellectual order and control on all we see around us. As we climb the concept mountain, our intellectual structures assume higher and higher levels of order. Nature is sliding down a pyramid of disorder, while our mental world is climbing up one. As the physical world decays, our conceptual world grows. At some level, it almost appears as if the decay of the physical world is being transformed into the expansion of the psychical world. Perhaps this is the greatest transformation of all – physical disorder transforming into higher and higher levels of intellectual order. A theoretical end-point for such a process would be a physical universe close to heat death, but with man's spirit and intellect having already escaped from its physical prison to some seventh heaven.

The Great Thinkers

The spearhead of man's responses came from five groups of great thinkers - artists, scientists, mathematicians, philosophers and prophets. A recent visit to the Church of Santa Croce in Florence[41] illustrated the point. Here one found the tombs and memorial plaques of many great men.

Santa Croce, Florence
Michelangelo, painter, sculptor, architect
Leonardo da Vinci, painter, inventor
Dante, writer
Rossini, composer
Galileo, scientist, astronomer
Marconi, inventor of the wireless
Fermi, scientist, mathematician
Bruno, humanist
Michaelius, scientist, naturalist
Machiavelli, advisor to the popes
Many eminent Churchmen

Truly a cathedral of some of the greatest thinkers. It is they who helped develop much of the conceptual repertoire that underpins our civilisation. They are the spearhead of our intellectual evolution. Their great minds have contributed much towards defining and developing our understanding of man's strange predicament. Above all, they are driven by an overwhelming need to know and understand.

---

[41]   See: http://www.santacroce.firenze.it/
Image courtesy of en.wikipedia.org org

The Disciplines

The conceptual repertoire is usually divided into disciplines such as art, philosophy and science, but all of these disciplines have as common roots the different forms of response outlined above. That is their common thread. Each discipline has developed its own set of rules which help it to filter out the good from the bad. These rules are the equivalent of natural selection in the living world. With them, the conceptual repertoire of man became a self-organising system. Ideas are born, flourish, decay and die, like in all imperfection-driven systems.

Art

Artists represent nature in ever new ways and force us to constantly re-evaluate our emotional and intellectual relationship with it. Their representations are a way of taking possession of nature, importing it into our own mental framework where we can analyse and manipulate it.

It is difficult to define exactly what constitutes a work of art. Philosophers and thinkers in the realms of art and aesthetics have wrestled to find answers since the time of Aristotle and Plato. In trying to define the boundaries that differentiate a work of art from any other artefact, there are two main groups of characteristics; *intrinsic* - those that are properties of the object itself, and *subjective* - those that lie in the eye of the beholder.

Intrinsic criteria have traditionally included:

> The object must be an artefact, an object *deliberately* created by an artist.

> It should be an original, not a copy of something else.

It should exhibit a high level of technical skill within its chosen medium

Here are a few commonly accepted *subjective* criteria:

A work-of-art should be deemed have outstanding aesthetic merit.
It should have *form,* a meaningful structure, not a piece of chaos.
It should have symbolic meaning, conveying a hidden message.
Its message should be delivered with economy.
It should appeal to the soul.
It should model nature, and provide insight into its forms, structures and ideas.

The role of the artist is therefore to help us to *understand* our imperfect world, *model* it in another medium, *interpret* its hidden messages and *realign* our attitudes towards it.

The aim of art is to represent not the outward appearance of things, but their inward significance.

- Aristotle

The world today doesn't make sense, so why should I paint pictures that do?"

- Picasso[42]

A subject that is beautiful in itself gives no suggestion to the artist. It lacks imperfection.

- Oscar Wilde[43]

---

[42] Pablo **Picasso**, 1881-1973. Spanish painter and sculptor, one of the greatest and most influential artists of the 20th century, widely known for co-founding the Cubist movement

[43] Oscar **Wilde,** 1854-1900. Irish writer / playwright

> *To banish imperfection is to destroy expression, to check exertion, to paralyze vitality.*
>
> - John Ruskin[44]

> *The artist who aims at perfection in everything achieves it in nothing.*
>
> - Eugene Delacroix[45]

Science

The objective of science is master, control and predict our physical environment. To this end scientists seek out the laws that lie behind every natural phenomenon. We have bought into the idea that a rational explanation exists for every physical and even mental phenomenon and we turn to the scientist to help us understand and control it. Science promises us a comfort zone where we are, or can be, in control of our environment. We have a deep felt need for such control.

> *It is the function of art to disturb us. It is the function of science to reassure us.*
>
> - Georges Braque [46]

One of the important leaps forward was the discovery of the scientific method. This consisted of forming a hypothesis or model of how some natural phenomenon worked, then devising a set of experiments to prove or disprove the hypothesis. A proven hypothesis becomes a law of science. This may seem rather obvious to us now, but until its

---

[44] John **Ruskin**, 1819-1900. English art critic. *The Stones of Venice*.

[45] Ferdinand Victor Eugène **Delacroix**, 1798-1863. French artist, regarded as the leader of the French Romantic school

[46] Georges **Braque,** 1982-1963. French painter, invented cubism with Picasso

formulation around the 16th century no real progress in science and technology was possible.

Galileo was one of the first to implement the scientific method. At his time, general wisdom was that a heavy object such as a stone fell to the ground faster than a lighter object such as a feather. Galileo devised a set of experiments to test this belief. Tradition has it that he dropped heavy and light objects from the top of the Leaning Tower of Pisa and recorded the results. He proved that all objects will fall at the same speed if secondary effects such as wind resistance are eliminated. The acceleration due to gravity is independent of the weight of the body. With Galileo's experiments modern science was born.

The role of the scientist is thus to help us *understand* and *model* the many phenomena we observe in nature, leading us to be able to *control* and *exploit* these phenomena. Turning science inward on ourselves we learn more about how we function and how we relate to everything else.

> *The greatest discoveries of science have always been those that forced us to rethink our beliefs about the universe and our place in it.*
>
> *- L. Park*[47]

Mathematics

Slowly it is beginning to dawn on us that our minds were constructed to deal only with the very special conditions that exist in our own

---

[47]   Robert Lee **Park**, b.1931 American physicist, professor of physics at University of Maryland.

world. They were not designed to deal with anything outside this box. As science progresses we begin to find that ultimate reality bears little relationship to what we perceive it to be. Our everyday minds are not geared to handle such abstract ideas as special relativity or quantum physics.

The only way we can cope with this is through mathematics. We can build mathematical models to represent this strange universe, and we can manipulate its symbols as if they were something real, even if they represent something far beyond the reach of our everyday imagination.

Mathematics has become a medium that helps us connect with that other strange world. Our models of this world become more and more abstruse, understood only by the greatest mathematicians. When our scientists claim to view ultimate reality, what they are looking at on many occasions is a mathematical equation. Some phenomena exist just as mathematical equations such as the behaviour of the fundamental particles, space and its multiple dimensions, and the existence of alternative universes.

The equations of mathematics could themselves be disconnected from ultimately reality and we may never be able to prove otherwise. We could be looking at reality through a distorted lens. However it is the only such lens that we have got. In mathematics we have a remarkable tool to help us build our internal *models* of the world. But it is not a route to absolute truth as some would have us believe. Mathematics is not immune to the virus of flaws.

As far as the laws of mathematics refer to reality, they are not certain; and as far as they are certain, they do not refer to reality.

- Einstein

Philosophy

The aim of philosophy is to provide an intellectual framework within which we can view and debate the world. It is philosophers who ask the fundamental questions, often questions that are impossible to answer.

-About Self:

I am thinking. I am conscious of myself thinking. How do I know that I am thinking? Who/what is doing the thinking? Who am I? Why am I here in this strange dilemma in the first place? Who put me here? What is life? What is death? What comes after...?

-About the World

Why is there something out there instead of nothing? Has it any purpose? Had it a beginning? Who thought it all up? Why is it the way it is...?

-Self and the World

Does the world really exist or is it just a figment of my imagination? Can I prove it really exists? The images in my mind, do they really exist? Do they bear any relationship with what actually exists outside? Can I trust my knowledge of the world? Could it be deceiving me? Am I part of this world or am I something else...?

-Nature of man

Do we have free will or is this an illusion? Why have we a sense of good and evil...?

The role of philosophy is to pose these questions, ones of profound interest to us all. It does not purport to provide hard answers. Its conclusions are not subject to any form of rigorous proof. It is not science. Rather its aim is to provide a vocabulary and a methodology with which to debate these big questions. It provides a process, rather than an end result.

The philosopher does not aim to solve practical or theoretical problems; he does not deliver any useful artefacts. He does not claim to provide hard answers even to philosophical questions. The flaws or intellectual gaps he is addressing are very fundamental and hard answers may never be found. But philosophy provides a valuable service in posing these questions and providing a framework for their debate. In short, the philosopher's role is to help us to *understand*, to *interpret* and to *realign*.

Religions

When ancient man was threatened by nature through disease, natural calamity, conflicts and adversity, he turned to the gods for protection. He interpreted nature's threats as signs of the wrath of God against mankind and initiated the ritual of sacrifice to appease this wrath. To overcome the greatest threat of all – death – he developed concepts of an afterlife at a very early stage. The many burial mounds with their elaborate preparations for the journey across the great divide bear witness to the beliefs of our ancestors.

Later emerged the prophets who developed elaborate codes of conduct to guide man in his wayward ways and lead him to a higher form of existence. Many religions are based on the teachings of great prophets, who their followers believe had profound moral insight and spoke through divine inspiration. Their vision of the afterlife promised the ultimate aim of escaping from the constraints of this world and conquering death.

Each religion provides us with its own answers to the basic questions - the origin of the cosmos, the nature of God, man's purpose, his final destination and the afterlife. They have provided a rich harvest of concepts which are valued by millions of people and which have a profound effect on their practical and spiritual lives. Religion provides positive answers in areas where science cannot access and has no tools to penetrate. Man's spiritual response is driven by many deeply-felt needs - a desire for protection against a hostile world, a feeling of being a flawed creature, a desire to escape from this unhappy world, a need to conquer mortality and a need for some ultimate vision of perfection.

Religious acceptance relies on faith, a form of belief in which many millions of people participate, people who find that it answers many of their deepest needs. In our attempts to *understand, interpret, realign and escape*, it provides a totally different route to that provided by science. It is a route favoured by a vast number of people.

Social Science

The growth of ideas brought a parallel growth in the structure of society. Complexity grew as many large scale and powerful organisations began to appear. Society has always been a battle ground between conformity and diversity. Individual freedom, however laudable, if carried to extremes can threaten the common good of a whole society. Curbs have to be put in place. The proper balance between individual freedom and common good is something every society has been seeking to attain.

Organisations or movements based on specified political, social or religious beliefs are often termed *isms*; they have usually arisen to promote conformity of a large number of people to some ideal or way of thinking. Some examples are:

Political
Feudalism, Imperialism, Fascism, Nationalism, Racism, Socialism, Communism, Maoism, Colonialism

Religious
Catholicism, Clericalism, Protestantism, Lutheranism. Evangelism, Confucianism

Economic
Capitalism, Consumerism, Marxism, Monetarism

Voluntary
Trade Unionism, Feminism, Environmentalism, Conservationism

Many isms have been benevolent in nature, often starting off with a high degree of idealism. However some were hijacked by ruthless leaders in search of power and ended up as being extremely repressive. In some societies, non-conformity to the prevailing ism was punishable by torture and death.

Human behaviour ranges across many extremes, from very good to the very bad. The dilemma of society is how to deal with the bad without suppressing the good at the same time. It is the role of the social sciences to find a workable balance.

Consilience

E.O.Wilson[48] has written persuasively on the need for consilience, the unification of the many main branches of learning. He uses the term *consilience* to denote the coming together of the many varied disciplines which currently occupy our intellectual life. He has noted the lack of a common language and theoretical basis between the hard sciences, the social sciences, art, philosophy and religion and postulates that one of the greatest intellectual challenges of our time lies in bringing together into a coherent framework these many divergent disciplines.

> *The ongoing fragmentation of knowledge and the resulting chaos in philosophy are not reflections of the real world but artefacts of scholarship.*

At their most basic level the disciplines have all the same origin - the intellect's attempts to come to terms with itself and its flawed environment. This may be their common theoretical basis. In an earlier chapter, the intellect's responses were classified under the headings *understanding, modelling, mastery, exploitation,*

---

[48] Edward O. **Wilson,** b1929, American Biologist, Pulitzer Prize 1978, *Consilience,(1998)*

93

interpretation, realignment and escape. Each discipline contributes as follows:

Art	*Understand, model, interpret, realign*
Science	*Understand, model, master, exploit*
Philosophy	*Understand, interpret, realign*
Religion	*Interpret, realign, escape*

No one discipline supplies all the answers. They are all different windows through which people observe the same thing – the mystifying and magical world we live in.

Summary

Starting from the first appearance of life, nature took 4 billion years in preparation for the arrival of for consciousness. These were years of trial and error, categorised by ever increasing sophistication and complexity. Complexity reached its peak with the development of the human brain. How the transition occurred between intelligence and consciousness remains one of the greatest mysteries.

Once arrived, consciousness became aware that it lived in an imperfect dwelling. It had an overwhelming need to understand this place – how it worked and why. It proceeded to model the world using its powers of abstract thought. Eventually it mastered most of its dwelling place and could manipulate it at will.

It was driven by imperfection. In a state of perfect knowledge and understanding, the disciplines that consciousness created in its attempts to model the world would never have been needed.

Chapter 7.
LEANING TOWERS

Around 1173, the citizens of Pisa began constructing a tower, designed to be one of the most beautiful towers in the world. Before the tower was completed, it began to tilt. It had been built on faulty foundations. The builders continued to build and finished one the

world's great masterpieces. The leaning slowly got worse until the tower was in danger of complete collapse and had to be closed. Dozens of ideas were put forward as to how to put it right. Not until 1990 was a solution found that succeeded in partially correcting the leaning and enabling the tower to be reopened to the public. It remains to this day, a beautiful but flawed symbol of a great ideal.

The Leaning Tower of Pisa[49]

---

[49]   Image from Wikipedia Commons. Author: NotFromUtrecht 23 may 2012

Michael J Walsh, B.E., Ph.D

The Cathedral of Concepts

From the middle ages until the end of the 19ᵗʰ century, another beautiful structure was also being built, the cathedral of concepts. In this cathedral were wonderful works of art, deep philosophic discourses and the discoveries coming from the scientific revolution. The foundations on which it was built had much to do with perfection, a world view that had been developing since the time of Archimedes and Plato, reinforced by Galileo and Newton. These saw a world where order, purpose, harmony and perfection prevailed.

The architects were great minds like Michelangelo and Isaac Newton. Art flourished and the artist was revered as one endowed with divine inspiration. New levels of beauty and inspiration were achieved. In science, Newton's laws held supreme. They led to the belief that the world was based on simple, fixed laws and that, once these laws were known, man would be in control of everything. His equations would tell him everything he needed to know to predict and control nature. Behind everything there appeared a sense of purpose. Everything could be determined in advance. The movement of the stars, the emergence of life and the ascent of man all had a nice, neat inevitability about it. There was a grand plan, it was working beautifully and man was at its centre. The little wheels in the Swiss clock of nature were being mastered one by one, and a neat, synchronised model of everything was emerging. Mathematics flourished and gave the aura of complete certainty and perfect logic. Man now had the tools to tackle and tame any problem. His logic was unassailable.

At this time, the intellectual disciplines flourished. Mozart was writing symphonies in which one could not change a single note without

96

destroying the perfection of the whole conception. The greatest artists were engaged in creating works of wonderful visual beauty. Religion promised the idea of personal perfection in the sight of God. God's plan for a beautifully synchronised world was widely accepted, and an aura of perfect purpose prevailed. The poem, *The Tiger*, by Blake[50] summarized much of the current world view.

> TIGER, tiger, burning bright in the forests of the night,
> What immortal hand or eye could frame thy fearful symmetry?
> And what shoulder and what art could twist the sinews of thy heart?
> And, when thy heart began to beat, what dread hand and what dread feet?
>
> What the hammer? What the chain? In what furnace was thy brain?
> What the anvil? What dread grasp dare its deadly terrors clasp?
> When the stars threw down their spears and water'd heaven with their tears,
> Did He smile His work to see? Did He who made the lamb make thee?

The principles of design of this great cathedral were:

> The world was created according to some purposeful divine plan.
> The plan covered all of nature, living things, man himself and his eternal soul.
> God's purpose could be inferred from understanding this plan.
> Nature and all its resources were created as a gift to mankind.

---

[50]   William **Blake,** 1757–1827, English poet, painter, and printmaker.

The world is governed by beautiful, immutable laws.

These laws can be discovered by the intellect.

The intellect can lead man to towards ultimate truth.

In the end, man can escape the constraints of nature and go to a better place.

Life in this world is just a preparation for a perfect life in the next world.

At this time, all was right with the world of the intellect. The Age of Perfection was at its zenith. Nobody ever suspected that the whole structure might be built on a flawed foundation - perfection itself.

A new World View

Gradually it became clear that the real universe was built on an entirely different set of principles. Instead of order, there was disorder and diversity; instead of purpose, there was randomness; instead of harmony there was deadly competition; instead of perfection, there was imperfection. Gradually it became apparent that:

Man's intuition gave a totally false view of ultimate reality.

The real world was not anything like what it was envisaged it to be.

The galaxies, stars and our world were the result of a series of cosmic accidents.

Life grew out of inanimate matter by some rare chemical reaction.

Man, like all other forms of life, gradually evolved from very basic life forms.

Mans individuality is a result of random cell mutations.

There is no such thing as fixed time, fixed space.

Everything is relative to everything else. There are no absolutes.

The laws of nature that our intellect discovers are just approximations.

Scientific theories, while powerful, are subject to decay and death.

Even mathematics, once deemed to be absolute, is incomplete in itself.

The universe is fundamentally random and uncertain.

The great cathedral, like the leaning tower of Pisa, remained intact and still beautiful, but it too began to tilt. Many attempts are still being made to prop it up, but over time the battle will be lost.

Evolution

Blake posed the question, concerning the tiger:

What immortal hand or eye

Dare frame thy fearful symmetry?

Darwin's answer to Blake's question was not at all poetic and was quite shocking to many people. The tiger was not hammered out in some furnace in the sky. It was the result of millions of small accidents, spread out over billions of years. Each accident was insignificant at its time, but the cumulative effect added up to something remarkable. Man himself evolved in exactly the same way. The theory of evolution and natural selection arrived to stun a public which was well tuned to Blake's poetry. Many failed to see that an entirely new kind of poetry was being written.

Relativity

Euclid defined the space in which we live in terms of an elegant geometry. Space was just a big box made up of lines, triangles, circles and parabolas. Within this space the planets and stars moved with clocklike precision, observing Newton's beautiful Law of Gravitation. Most people could understand all this relatively easily. Then Einstein arrived. In one stroke, the mental models that had been built up over centuries were suddenly blown away. The real world did not at all conform to the images we had formed in our heads. There is no such thing as fixed time, it can speed up and slow down and even stop altogether. Distance is not fixed; it is a piece of elastic. Space is not three dimensions; it is four or maybe even eleven. Matter is a just another form of energy. The only absolute in our whole universe was the speed of light. Everything else is relative to this.

Our imaginations find it hard to cope with such a place. Our natural intuitions were giving us false pictures. The mental models we created were false. Mathematics was closer to reality. The only way to understand our universe was through mathematical equations. Where mathematics conflicted with our age old intuitions, it was mathematics that was always right. We had moved into a new era.

Playing Dice

As scientists delved deeper into the structure of matter, they were compelled to develop an entirely new kind of science. The tiny particles that make up matter - electrons, protons, muons - appeared to behave in very extraordinary ways. Their behaviour was random, and could not be predicted with any certainty. If you knew their position you could never measure their speed, and vice versa. It was as if they knew in advance that you were trying to measure them and they changed course in advance. Cause and effect, a fundamental basis of all science and everyday logic, seemed to be reversed. An electron can have multiple histories, and the history observed depends on the position of the observer. Heisenberg developed his famous Theory of Uncertainty to provide a mathematical model of what was happening. Einstein was horrified. He said: *God does not play dice with the universe.* Time would indicate that Heisenberg was right and Einstein wrong. As things developed, more and more throws of the dice were discovered.

The new science was quantum physics. It created a big dent in the idea of the universe as a giant Swiss watch, with perfectly interlocking parts. Chance and accident entered the picture. Quantum physics has steadily widened its remit. Other processes begin to show uncertainty as their basis.

A Multiverse

Worse was to come. Scientists began to conclude that there were billions of universes, created by some form of evolutionary or random process. Many of these universes would be hostile to life, but man has been just lucky to have arrived in this relatively benign one. This is the basis of the anthropic principle. Basically this says we got into the right universe by accident. Science went even further. It began to claim that the whole universe could have created itself spontaneously, possibly as a result of some unknown quantum effect. The very basis of creation was being challenged.

Incompleteness

All great thinkers are driven by a sense of incompleteness. The artist is filling some void in his or our understanding of the world. The scientist cannot tolerate some phenomenon that he cannot explain and is driven to express it in some form of law. The inventor observes a practical void in the lives of people and sets out to fill this. The philosopher's task is to debate and formalise the unknowable. The prophet addresses the mysteries of existence and provides answers to those searching to comprehend these. A sense of incompleteness drives all forward. Intuitively we sense that true completeness will never be achieved, as then all progress will cease.

The human mind thinks it can reach a perfect solution but it cannot. It seems to be making progress but perhaps it is just travelling in circles.

Mathematics

Many thought that mathematics was immune to uncertainty. From the time of Newton and the success of his elegant laws, scientists and philosophers concluded that all phenomena of the physical world could be incorporated into one comprehensive set of mathematical principles. This would be a completely self-contained logical system within which all proofs could be carried out by a set of mechanical rules and principles. This became the philosophy of determinism – all physical phenomena could be deduced from some set of absolute principles or formulae. Philosophy and speculation would become redundant. In the early 1900s, mathematicians like Bertrand Russell were frantically engaged in the development of such systems.

However in 1930 Gödel[51] showed that incompleteness extended into mathematics itself. He proved that mathematical systems were also incomplete and could lead to paradoxes just like the perfection paradox. His work shook the foundations of mathematics itself. The effort to develop universal mathematical systems collapsed overnight. Slipping away was the dream of a nicely synchronized universe obeying elegant laws, and supported by irrefutable mathematical logic. Imperfection was spreading. Gödel's theorem made a deep impact on the fields of mathematics and logic, and has been called the most significant mathematical truth of the 20th century.

The theorem can be stated in a number of ways:

Any effectively generated theory cannot be both consistent and complete at the same time.

In certain formal systems, there exist propositions that cannot be proved or disproved using the laws of that system.

It is impossible to prove within a consistent system that that system is consistent.

The theorem is the mathematical equivalent of the *liar paradox* in philosophy and logic. If a man says: *I am a liar*, do you believe him or not? Whichever course you choose, it leads to a paradox. In the end, a position must be taken; judgment must be exercised.

Russell's dream of creating a fully self-contained formal mathematical system foundered on the rocks of incompleteness. Gödel had

---

[51] Kurt Friedrich **Gödel**, 1906-1978. Austrian/American logician/ mathematician. *On Formally Undecidable Propositions (1930)*

effectively demonstrated that some mathematical propositions cannot be decided.

For example, Euclidean geometry is incomplete without the parallel assumption. It is not possible to prove or disprove the parallel assumption[52] from the remaining proofs. Therefore Euclid's *Elements* are incomplete in a logical sense. The missing logic must be provided from outside the system. We cannot solve the problem by widening the definition of system, since Gödel's theorem will still apply to the widened system.

Incompleteness has had many interpretations and consequences, some outside the field of formal mathematics for which initially devised it. Some of the interpretations are as follows:

> All logical systems of any complexity are incomplete. This applies to science, mathematics, logic, philosophy and other knowledge sciences. There systems, which are used to model the universe, are part of the universe as we ourselves are, and are thus *the system modelling itself.* They are therefore self-referential and incomplete. They cannot claim to be absolute.

> We cannot fully understand our own thinking, as this is the brain modelling itself. Again the results must be incomplete. The brain works computationally but the mind, in the form of consciousness, brings qualities such as judgment, understanding, imagination and vision. These qualities

---

[52] For more information, see http://en.wikipedia.org/wiki/parallel_postulate

are non-computational – they cannot be replicated on a computer – so Gödel's theory does not apply to these. A computer can replicate brain functions, but cannot replicate the qualities of consciousness.

Roger Penrose has commented as follows:

Gödel's result is that we ought not to ask, and cannot obtain, complete formalization of all thought processes. "Understanding" cannot be simulated in any kind of computational terms. The human faculty of being able to "understand" is something that must be achieved by some non-computational activity of the brain or mind. Human understanding and insight cannot be reduced to any set of computational rules.

Gödel's theorem argues that human insight lies beyond formal argument and beyond computable procedures. It serves also to illustrate the deeply mysterious nature of our mathematical perceptions. What the theorem actually tells us can be viewed positively, i.e. that the insights that are available to human mathematicians – indeed to anyone who can think logically with understanding and imagination – lie beyond anything that can be formalised as a set of rules. Rules can sometimes be a partial substitute for understanding, but can never replace it completely.

– Shadows of the Mind: A search for the Missing Science of Consciousness, 1991

Art

Incompleteness began to find its way into art. The sculptures of Henry Moore showing the human form full of holes and spaces, the paintings with random blobs on a page, modern classical music with no discernible shape or form – all these seem a long way from the beautifully structured works of the past. Many long for the good old days, but all that now seems to belong to a receding past.

Reclining Figure, 1951
Fitzwilliam Museum,
Cambridge.

Henry Moore [53]

What is happening here? One explanation is that modern artists are intuitively responding to incompleteness and imperfection. They no longer wish to dot every "i" and cross every "t". They deliberately leave holes and spaces. It is up to the observer or listener to fill in these holes and spaces. This makes him engage with the work of art instead of standing back and admiring it. He becomes part of the process itself. It is up to him to fill in the missing pieces. Imperfection draws him into the process.

I love playing modern music. It leaves lots of holes and spaces that the audience has to fill in for itself

- Le Yi Zhang.[54]

---

[53] Henry Spencer **Moore**, 1898-1986. English sculptor and artist. Image courtesy of en.wikipedia.org

[54] Le Yi **Zhang,** Chinese violinist. Nice, France

Theatre

The play *Waiting for Godot* was voted the best play of the 20th century[55]. The play opens with two tramps, Vladimir and Estragon, sitting on a heap of clay on which grows a single tree. They converse on various topics and reveal that they are waiting for a man named Godot. They do not know who Godot is or why he is coming or even if he will ever arrive. They just know that they have to wait for him.

> *But that is not the question. Why are we here, that is the question. And we are blessed in this, that we happen to know the answer. Yes, in this immense confusion one thing alone is clear. We are waiting for Godot to come.*

> *Let's go. Yes, let's go. (They do not move).*

As the play closes they are still waiting. Nothing has changed. Godot has not come, and we still do not know who he is or why he is coming. The play leaves many questions unanswered, but Beckett attempts no explanations. He leaves it to the audience to work out their own interpretation.

The author recently attended a piece of theatre in Nice. It was really a piece of anti-theatre. It broke every rule of what one expects theatre to be. It had no clear beginning. It began by one of the audience appearing to walk accidentally onto the stage. It was hard to differentiate the audience from the cast, as the actors seemed to emerge randomly from the audience. There was no plot or story.

---

[55] Play by Samuel Beckett, 1906-1989. Irish playwright/writer. Nobel Prize for literature 1969.

Most of the time when the actors began to speak, they seemed lost for words or mumbled unintelligible mumbo-jumbo. Lights switched on and off aimlessly. There were a few false endings, so it was hard to know when it was finally over. The audience was mystified. You could feel them working very hard to figure out what it was all about. There was a palpable response to what was *not* happening on the stage. It was a long way from the beautifully sculpted pieces of the past, yet it was an absorbing evening of theatre.

A passing thought:

Perhaps the audience was here before. In the theatre of life it had witnessed many marvellous spectacles. It watched the morning sun rise seemingly from out of the sea. It marvelled at the birth of a new child. It looked on and wondered. Since the dawn of consciousness, man has been trying to fill in the holes and spaces.

Social Systems

With newfound diversity of thought and the growing freedom of the individual, many of the leading isms lost their power and began to crumble. All isms require from their followers some degree of conformity to their stated beliefs and ideals. In the past, many of them introduced very severe sanctions against those who did not conform to these beliefs.

At political level, conformity was used as a very powerful tool in achieving control of a population. It is much easier to manipulate a homogenous population than an individualistic and heterogeneous one. Kings claimed that their power came from God and this justified them in enforcing conformity and obedience in whatever way they liked. This was called the Divine Right of Kings. Colonialism took control of many small nations and bent them to mirror the wishes of their conquerors.

Later came movements such as Communism and Nazism, which controlled populations with severe repression. Dictators such as Stalin and Hitler seized on ideological slogans such as *equality* and *racial purity* to justify torturing and killing millions of people.

At religious level, clerics who deemed they had ownership and control of *The Truth* felt they also had a duty to enforce it on all. Those who dissented were branded heretics. In the middle ages, powerful clerics used their power to torture and burn those who did not accept their interpretation of *The Truth*. One of the most powerful tools was to seize control of the sexual morality of a population. In this way, power extended into every home and bedroom.

To enforce conformity, many isms were compelled to impose severe sanctions. The sanctions imposed included fear, terror, social exclusion, prison, exile, torture, death, and eternal damnation. In The Museum of Man in San Diego[56] there is an exhibition of the hellish instruments of torture used by man against man. It is a disturbing reminder of the terrible price paid by people who dissented from the prevailing conformity.

Many institutions used concepts of perfection for the purposes of their own power. In enforcing conformity they were swimming against the tide of nature. Nature's way is diversity and experiment. Sooner

---

[56] www.museumofman.org/torture.

or later, it always wins out. Enforced conformity is in the long run no match for the power of nature's diversity.

In the modern world, one of the most powerful isms is consumerism. Many incentives are offered to induce people to spend more money and to buy particular products. People are not being forced, but they are subjected to many subtle influences. One result is that economic power tends to become concentrated into a small number of very powerful organisations. Many see this as the beginning of a new form of economic imperialism. If the organisations concerned do not use their power in a moral and just way, history tell us that they too will one day be swept away.

The Death of Certainty

As the new ideas spread, certainty began to slip away and uncertainty, chance and imperfection moved centre stage. The success of quantum theory in describing the quantum world and its deeply random behaviour, helped to drive the transition. The cult of perfection faded, and 2000 years of rainbow-chasing seemed to be coming to an end. Plato, with his very influential concepts of pre-design, perfection and absolutism, is now being accused (somewhat belatedly) of leading western thinking up a cul-de-sac for over 2000 years.

One is left with two radically different world views. One view is that the world is deterministic, that there is a definite plan behind it, underpinned by hard-wired laws and purpose. At the other extreme is the view that the world is completely random, has no specific purpose, and that everything that happens is the product of accident and chance.

It seems impossible to reconcile such different points of view. Perhaps there is a middle road. Could the universe have been deliberately created leaving holes and missing pieces, in order to force us into participating in the act of creation? If the Creator had made everything perfect and gave us perfect knowledge, we would have been reduced to the role of silent spectators.

Thoughts such as these lead us directly into the world of creation theories.

Chapter 8.
CREATION THEORIES

The perfection/imperfection debate inevitably brings us into the big questions of existence - the origins of the universe, of life, of man, and the existence of good and evil. A huge literature exists on these subjects, coming from religious leaders, philosophers and scientists. There are many competing theories. These fall mainly into two categories: God-based and-science based. The two categories appear to be mutually exclusive. Various attempts have been made to reconcile them, but a convincing common ground has yet to be found. The stumbling block has to do with perfection.

God-based theories include divine creation, creationism, and intelligent design. They imply the existence of a perfect, all-powerful Creator. Science- based theories include evolutionism, M-Theory and various theories of everything. These postulate that our universe is controlled by internal forces which can be entirely explained by science. These theories are discussed in outline below. Of particular interest is in the role played by perfection and imperfection within each theory.

Divine Creation

Many faiths believe that the universe and everything in it was created by an all-knowing, all-powerful God. Different religions have different visions of what this God is, but a common theme among them is the association of godliness with perfection. Here are a few of the most important views:

> The *ancient Greeks* had 12 Gods, living on the top of Mount Olympus. Their gods were not at all perfect. They made mistakes but they atoned for them. The Greeks practiced polytheism, i.e. multiple gods, while developments elsewhere were based on monotheism, i.e. one single god.

> The *Christian* religion commenced in Palestine, with the birth of Jesus Christ. It taught of a personal God consisting of three persons, the creator of the world and the redeemer of mankind. Knowledge of God has come through the process of revelation, a direct manifestation of divine will or truth. Thomas Aquinas summarized the attributes of this God as *simplicity, perfection, goodness, incomprehensibility, omnipresence, immutability, eternity and oneness*. Belief in God is a question of personal faith, and has nothing to do with science or experimental proof. Man is viewed as a fallen creature, attributed to his past sins, and God became incarnate on earth in the form of Jesus Christ, in order to redeem man from his sins.

> *Creation science* attempts to provide a scientific basis for creation using texts from the Bible and the writings of the prophets. The methodology used has been discredited by both the scientific community and the mainstream churches.

In *Judaism,* the concept of God is strictly monotheistic. God is incomprehensible and unknowable. He is an absolute being who is the ultimate cause of all existence. He is a spirit, personal, all-powerful, eternal, holy and compassionate. God interacts with mankind and the world. The Creator is the same person as the God of Abraham who delivered the Israelites from slavery in Egypt, and led them to the Promised Land.

In *Islam,* there is One True God – Allah. According to Islamic belief, Allah is the proper name of God, and humble submission to his will and commandments is the pivot of the Muslim faith. Allah is the only God, creator of the universe, and the judge of humankind. He is unique and inherently all-merciful and omnipotent. The Qur'an is the word of God, revealed to Mohammad through the archangel Gabriel.

Buddhism is mostly atheistic, but does not deny the existence of beings that might be called gods. Salvation can be won only through the human mind. Buddha was not a god and did not claim to be. He taught how to live a moral life and eventually reach perfect peace and tranquility.

In Hinduism, Brahman is a supreme, universal spirit, the origin and essence of all existence. Rather than believing in one personal God, most Hindus believe that all reality – gods, the universe, human beings and all else – is essentially one thing. All share the same essence. Brahmin cannot be seen or heard but its nature can be known only through intense meditation. Hindus worship many gods, but they are seen as many masks of Brahman.

In *Taoism*, Tao is the unified something from which all things arise. It is not a personal creator but an unseen force that is the origin and order of the universe. It is beyond the reach of intellectual knowledge. It pervades the natural world, constantly ordering and nurturing it. All parts of the universe are in harmony and human beings are part of this harmony. People should live in harmony with the Tao.

In *Baha'i,* God is the supernatural creator. He is an unknowable, divine being who has revealed himself through nine leaders: Moses, Buddha, Confucius, Jesus, Mohammad, and their founders. Baha'i emphasizes the unity of all religions and peoples.

For *Pantheists*, God resides in nature without a separate existence. Pantheism is the belief that the universe and all of nature is identical with divinity, or that everything composes an all-encompassing, immanent God. Pantheists thus do not believe in a distinct personal god. Eastern religions are often considered to be pantheistically inclined.

A fundamental difference between different religions relates to the existence of a personal God, a God with whom man can have a personal relationship. Christianity, Judaism, and Islam hold this belief; the universe was created for a purpose and man himself lies at the centre of this purpose; man can have a special relationship with this God. Other religions see God as impersonal and not accessible to humans.

The Soul

The presence of a distinct human soul, separate from the body, is a key element in the teaching of many religions. The soul can achieve perfection, usually by mastering the imperfections inherent in man's base nature. The soul is the seat of goodness and the other virtues. It was created by God, is eternal, and will find its eventual home with God. Underlying these beliefs is the view that the human soul can perfect itself in this life in preparation for the next.

In *Christianity*, the soul is eternal and goes to either heaven or hell depending on how one lives one's life. Physical resurrection on Last Day is promised.

Judaism does not have an official credo but many believe in an eternal soul, destined to live with God or else in eternal suffering. There is eventual physical resurrection.

In *Islam,* Muslims must submit to the will of God to gain paradise after death. Hell awaits the evil-doers.

In *Buddhism*, people do not have a soul or spirit as such. There is a cycle of rebirth whereby one is reborn into one of many possible realms. People can escape the cycle of rebirth by reaching nirvana, a state of spiritual perfection. A person carries his or her karma forward to the next reincarnation. Karma means deeds and people can influence their karma by their present moral actions.

Hinduism teaches a continuous cycle of reincarnation until liberation from the constraints of the human condition is achieved. Liberation is an experience characterized by infinite being, infinite awareness and infinite bliss. Hinduism offers three paths to liberation – good works, knowledge and devotion. There is a concept of karma very similar to that of Buddhism.

Taoism has little to say on what happens after death or about an afterlife. In this respect Taoism has much in common with Confucianism. It regards death as a return from life back to the original unity of the Tao.

In *Baha'i,* souls are immortal; nearness to God is heaven; remoteness from God is hell. Heaven and hell are states of being, not places.

The soul is a key element in the human search for perfection. Art and music are deemed to come from the soul, as are many of the attributes of consciousness such as wisdom, enlightenment and goodness.

Intelligent Design

This postulates that the current state of life on earth has come about through the actions of an intelligent designer, and not by evolution. Some aspects of the universe show positive evidence of being the result of an intelligent cause. For example, some living things exhibit a level of complexity that cannot be explained solely by evolution. The living cell, for example, is deemed irreducibly complex in that it could not have evolved from a simpler state because that simpler state would not have worked or served any function. The designer need not be God, but most followers clearly have God in mind. Critics say that intelligent design is creationism by another name.

Evolution

Evolutionists contend that the development of life on earth and the emergence of man were the results of processes such as mutation and natural selection. Darwin was a rigorous scientist and was careful to point out that the theory of evolution did not apply to the *emergence* of life on earth, only to its subsequent development. He recognised how special an event the emergence of life was. Few now dispute Darwin's theories, including many church leaders.

A Theory of Everything

The Holy Grail of science is to find a Theory of Everything (TOE), one concise, integrated theory that contains within itself all the equations of the physical universe. If such a theory could describe the behaviour of the entire physical universe, it would be a huge leap forward in our understanding. If it went further and accounted for the actual creation of our universe, then it would come very close to the mind of the Creator.

The most promising current candidate is M-Theory. It has evolved from string theory which in turn is based on quantum theory. In quantum theory, randomness and chance play a dominant role, so the universe of M-theory is fundamentally random. There is no element of purpose or determinism in its solution. Of M-Theory, Stephen Hawking[57] has written:

> *Because there is a law like gravity, the universe can and will create itself from nothing... Spontaneous creation is the reason why there is something rather than nothing, why the universe exists, why we exist. It is not necessary to invoke God to light the blue touch paper and set the universe going.......M-Theory is the only candidate for*

---

[57] Stephen William **Hawking** ; 1942-, English physicist, *The Grand Design*

a complete theory of the universe. If it is finite – and this has yet to be proved – it will be a model of a universe that creates itself... If the theory is confirmed by observation, it will be a successful conclusion of a search going back 3,000 years. We will have found the grand design.

M-Theory is a complex mathematical formulation, understood by only a handful of scientists. It is not yet complete and may prove unverifiable by experiment. Many are sceptical of the claim that science is close to finding the secret of creation.

To know the history of science is to recognize the mortality of any claim to universal truth.

- Evelyn Fox Keller

Science, like life, feeds on its own decay. New facts burst old rules; then newly divined conceptions bind old and new together into a reconciling law.

- William James

Science is all those things which are confirmed to such a degree that it would be unreasonable to withhold one's provisional consent.

- Stephen Jay Gould

Science, in the very act of solving problems, creates more of them.

- Abraham Flexner

Science and Religion

It is worthwhile to try and isolate the exact points of departure between science and religion. At first glance, one would think that there should be room for both.

Science

There are areas where many scientists admit that they can never penetrate. The tools of science have no validity before time and the universe began. Totally different rules and conditions may have existed before then. Even if the universe created itself spontaneously, there is no theory as to what triggered the event, or why.

Many suspect that the mysteries surrounding human existence and consciousness will remain forever beyond the reach of science. These mysteries could well be the work of God. But many scientists cannot accept this, citing that they cannot have a scientific proof that God exists and actually did these things. They prefer to believe, and perhaps hope, that science may one day make radical new discoveries which will answer all these questions. This is a form of scientific fundamentalism, a sticking to the letter of scientific law, to the exclusion of all other possibilities. It is an act of faith in the assumed infallibility of human reasoning.

Richard Dawkins in his book *The God Delusion*[58] regards religious belief as a delusion and believes that modern science has made the concept of God redundant. Some of his quotes are as follows:

---

[58]   Richard **Dawkins** is an evolutionary biologist, and author of *The God Delusion 2006*. Also *The Selfish Gene 1976*

I am against religion as it teaches us to be satisfied with not understanding the world.... Be thankful that you have a life, and forget your vain and presumptuous desire for a second one... Religion is about turning untested belief into unshakable truth through the power of institutions and the passage of time.... There is real poetry in the real world. Science is the poetry of reality.

Other scientists take a different view.

In comparing religious belief to science, I try to remember that science is belief also.

- Robert Brault[59]

The most beautiful and most profound experience is the sensation of the mystical. It is the sower of all true science. He to whom this emotion is a stranger, who can no longer wonder and stand rapt in awe, is as good as dead. To know that what is impenetrable to us really exists, manifesting itself as the highest wisdom and the most radiant beauty which our dull faculties can comprehend only in their primitive forms - this knowledge, this feeling is at the centre of true religiousness.

- Albert Einstein *"The Merging of Spirit and Science"*

Religion

On the religious side there have also been elements of fundamentalism. Different religions have teachings often deemed to be the direct word of God as revealed by the prophets and therefore

---

[59] Robert **Brault**, American free-lance writer, contributor to magazines and newspapers in the USA for over 40 years. Connecticut USA. http://www. robertbrault.com/

beyond dispute. For example, the Bible states that God created the world in 6 days. How is this to be taken? What is meant by a day in this context? Is there any room for interpretation of what such a day might mean? Is this a statement of scientific fact? If the latter stance is taken, then there is a head-on collision with science.

The collision of the early church with Galileo arose from precisely this position. Galileo did not dispute the existence or power of God. His discovery was deemed to be at variance with Holy Scripture. The Holy Tribunal set up by the church to try Galileo concluded:

> *The proposition that the sun is the centre of the world and does not move from its place is absurd and false philosophically and formally heretical, because it is expressly contrary to Holy Scripture.*

Galileo's response was:
> *The Bible shows the way to Heaven, not the way the heavens go.*

Galileo was placed under house arrest until his death in 1760. A ban was put on printing his works. In 1992 the Vatican formally and publicly cleared Galileo of any wrong-doing. Galileo's remains lie in the Santa Croce Basilica in Florence. On his tomb is clearly depicted a sun-centred solar system.

Good and Evil
Religions often have difficulty in explaining the presence of imperfection in God's creation. Man can behave as a fallen creature, capable of dreadful deeds. There is lot of evil evident in the world. After a big natural disaster, where thousands of people may have been killed, people often ask how a perfect, loving God could have

permitted such a disaster to visit his people. The answers to these questions are often far from convincing. The stumbling block is how an all-perfect god could be involved in something ostensibly imperfect. Even Einstein, an avowed atheist, had difficulty with this paradox. He could not tolerate the imperfections and randomness inherent in a scientific theory such as quantum physics. He felt that God would not have created the world that way.

If religion has difficulty in explaining the presence of *evil,* equally evolutionists have difficulty in explaining the presence of *goodness.* Goodness, in its many manifestations, does not fit comfortably into a theory based on competition and survival of the fittest. It is hard to explain it as some kind of pre-programmed biological mechanism. Its opposite, in the form of selfishness and egocentrism, fits much better.

The religious view that goodness is something fundamental to human consciousness and the human soul is more acceptable to the vast majority of people.

Bye-Bye Perfection

In the various theories of creation, the idea of perfection frequently lies hidden beneath the surface. The universe is either the work of a perfect Creator, or the outcome of some perfect equation. Either scenario leads to many paradoxes and anomalies.

It is time to jettison perfectionism and the fundamentalism that often accompanies it. Imperfection, with its acceptance of incompleteness and uncertainty, is a much better way forward.

Michael J Walsh, B.E., Ph.D

Plato, turn in your grave!

> *Science and religion are two windows that people look through,*
> *trying to understand the big universe outside, trying to understand*
> *why we are here. The two windows give different views, but both*
> *look out at the same universe. Both views are one-sided, neither is*
> *complete. Both leave out essential features of the real world. And*
> *both are worthy of respect*
>
> *- Freeman Dyson[60]*

---

[60] Freeman John **Dyson**, b.1923 Berkshire, England. British/American physicist and mathematician.

Chapter 9.
IMPERFECTION IN ACTION

When we look at all of creation we never cease to wonder at its variety and diversity. We see the heavens with billions of stars and galaxies of every imaginable kind, our own world of constantly changing landscapes, the teeming life of the forests and not least the seemingly limitless world of the human mind. We wonder how it all came about and what engine is at work to create this magnificent diversity and complexity.

There is a very simple answer, so simple that it has been overlooked by everybody - *imperfection*. It is imperfection, and the various responses that it has invoked, that have created the diversity of the universe.

Imperfection has extraordinary powers but it hides them well. It operates by proxy. It achieves its objectives by creating a web of disturbance and uncertainty. It then, like the spider, lies in wait for the responses. It has infinite patience. It knows that by hiding in the wings, success will inevitably come its way. While its actions may appear random and unpredictable, it gives the impression of knowing where it is going.

Imperfection wants you to dislike it, to have a negative reaction to it. The harder you try to eliminate it, the more imperfection you spread. The last thing imperfection wants is that you accept the status quo and do nothing. It wants you to react. Think of the thousands of artefacts that have resulted from our response to bad and unpredictable weather. These may solve the weather problem but they create a new range of problems. In modern society, housing has long replaced the weather as a source of distress.

The amazing universe in which we live, with all its things, happenings, thoughts, and imaginings, can be traced back through millennia of small questions and answers. Imperfection asks its questions and then lies in wait for the responses. These responses have already yielded the stunning heavens of galaxies, stars and planets; the wonderful diversity of living creatures; the never-ending attempts to organise human society and the extraordinary achievements of the human mind. Not a bad harvest for an unloved fellow-traveller.

Seeking Reactions
It is the reaction to disturbances that drives nature's processes.

In the universe, it is nature's response to imbalances in the distribution of matter, energy and heat that drives the galaxies, creates the stars and heats the earth.

With living things, natural selection filters out the good disturbances from the bad and the result is the marvellous diversity of living things.

The more poorly that man behaves, the more new systems – social, legal and religious - are put in place to confine and restrain him. These very systems create opportunities for even more sophisticated forms of misbehaviour. As constraints get tougher, the mischievous get smarter.

The world of ideas has been a graveyard for many seemingly good concepts. Good ideas flower for a while but soon decay. Their very decay spawns more ideas which in turn join the cycle of decay. Man's response to the constant decay of ideas has spawned the ever-evolving worlds of science, mathematics, art and philosophy.

Asking Questions

Max Planck, the eminent scientist, once said: *An experiment is a question which science poses to nature, and a measurement is the recording of nature's answer.* One can restate the role of imperfection in somewhat similar fashion: *A disturbance is a question posed by imperfection. The result, positive or negative, is a recording of the environment's response.*

Big questions are never asked, only millions of little ones. Nature's way is to ask a small question, await the answer for whatever time it takes, and then move on to the next question. A tiger is the result of millions of small questions asked over millions of years. Each little question was relatively easy to answer at the time but the cumulative result is something stunning. Every tiger is a different experiment. We don't see all the failed experiments. All that is left for us to see are the surviving ones. The entire world we see around us is a recording of the disturbances which have survived. It is Nature's front window, not its back yard.

The Answers

Newton's law of motion, as applied to physical phenomena, states:

> To every action there is an equal and opposite reaction.

The Le Chatelier[61] principle, used in chemistry, states:

> Any change in status quo prompts an opposing reaction in the responding system.

Chaos Theory states:

> Small, localized perturbations in one part of a complex system can have widespread consequences throughout the system.

The disturbance/response model thus occurs in nature in many guises.

The Agent of Change

One can confidently make the bold statement that *all change* is imperfection-driven. Perfection is complete in itself and does not require any change. It has no need to alter the status quo. So it follows, almost by definition, that all systems that exhibit change are driven by imperfection. Imperfection itself does not directly drive things forward. It is neutral and random and has no specific goals. However its presence inevitably invokes response mechanisms. These provide the filters that separate the good from the bad.

---

[61] Henri Louis **Le Châtelier**, 1850-1936. An influential French chemist

An Example

The following is a trivial example which helps to illustrate imperfection in action. Afterwards the concept will be generalised.

A catering manager in a large hotel has devised a system for laying out the dining room, designing the menu, taking customer orders and arranging payment. He documents all of this in a system manual and expects everybody to follow this. However there are many deviations in the way the staff follow the laid down procedures. These arise from pressure of work, laziness, disobedience or other human frailty.

Some of the deviations turn out to be good, others bad. The customers make their judgments and quickly let their responses be known, be they favourable or unfavourable.

Bad deviations are quickly discarded. Good ones are approved and adopted for future use. The system manual is changed. It becomes the systems' memory bank, incorporating all the successful deviations to date. The individual deviations may be small and simple, but their cumulative effect is something quite complex. The above cycle repeats itself many times. The efficiency of the hotel improves with every new cycle and the hotel becomes famous for the quality of its service.

The Model

The generalised model runs as follows:

A system such as described above runs in cycles. The cycles are initiated by some disturbance or perceived imperfection. They all run according to a similar logic.

The model is given in the diagram below. It is worth spending a little time on this as it will be used later to analyse a whole range of systems.

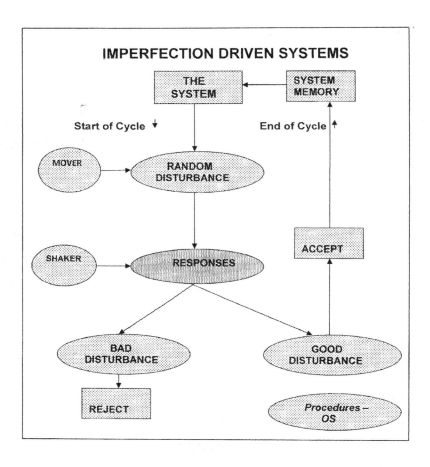

The components of the model are as follows:

The System

Any group of inter-connected things and processes can be looked at as a system. A system is often imagined as being a kind of imaginary box. Things within the box interact with each other in various ways, and can be studied in isolation. Sometimes events originating outside the box happen to influence what happens inside.

Systems can be nested within other systems, like boxes within boxes, each influencing the other. Our universe consists of a large number of interconnected systems - the cosmos, the earth, the living world, the human race etc. These are all dynamic systems, subject to constant flux and change. They are evolving towards some new state.

Rules and Procedures

Every system has its rules and procedures. These are invisible, like the operating system in a computer. They tell each element of the system what to do and when to do it. They are designed to handle every eventuality, like disturbances and chance events. They determine the entire dynamics and final destination of the system.

The Disturbance

Disturbances occur within a system. They are usually random and upset the prevailing equilibrium. They are neutral and have no particular objective. They may be may be good or bad, negative or positive. Some improve the system, while others harm it. The system has now changed - for better or worse.

The Mover

The disturbance is initiated by some agent or other, the *mover*. The identity of the mover is often hard to establish. We do not know for example the identity of the mover who created the first disturbances and imbalances in the infant universe.

The Response

The disturbance demands a response. It is like a discord in music. It cries out to be resolved. A filter is needed to distinguish a good disturbance from a bad one. A good disturbance will last a long time before its flaws appear. A bad disturbance displays its flaws very quickly and will soon disappear. The quality of a disturbance can be measured by its *gain*, the amount of time it takes to find out its flaws.

> Someone has suggested that the salaries of people in a business should be proportional to the length of time it takes for their mistakes to be found out. The operator on the shop floor will have his mistakes found out in minutes. The managing director may make strategic decisions whose flaws may not appear for decades.

The Shaker

The responses are initiated by what will be called the *shaker*. The shaker is independent of the original mover. Its task is to filter out the bad disturbances and consolidate the good ones by encoding them in the system memory.

In the field of evolution, the environment is the shaker. It is where the response of natural selection begins. It tests new mutations and filters out the negative ones. A defective tiger will have no offspring and may be killed or starve to death. Equally effective measures are employed in other systems.

The Cycle

After a disturbance there is a changed system. At times a sense of equilibrium may appear to have been reached. But perfection has not been reached. A perfect system, one where no further improvement can be envisaged, is just one whose flaws have not yet been discovered. Inevitably flaws emerge. Then the cycle starts all over again.

Exiting the Cycle

In the hotel example given earlier, a point may be reached where further improvements cannot be implemented due to constraints such as lack of space or unavailability of trained staff. The hotel may have to rebuild or relocate elsewhere. There is now a totally new framework. A new system with a different operating cycle and a whole new set of procedures will commence. An event such as this is termed a *transition*. Some important transitions have taken place in nature.

System Memory

A key component is system memory. Here all successful disturbances are recorded for passing on to the next cycle. In a living organism, all past experience is encoded in its DNA and this is passed on to the next generation. Without a system memory, all past experience would be lost. A faulty memory could result in chaos in the succeeding cycles.

Self-Organisation

Once the rules and processes are laid down, the system runs itself from there on. There is no need for continuous intervention as long as the rules are being observed.

Application of the Model

The imperfection-driven model can be applied to the major systems addressed in earlier chapters. These include:

System	Chapter	Paragraph
Physical Systems		
A model of a multiverse	3	Imperfection Arrives
The formation of our universe	4	Setting up our world
Living World		
Theory of Evolution	4	Evolution
Human systems		
Development of tools and devices	5	Physical – The Response
The conceptual repertoire	6	Responses to the Environment
The Internet	5	Mental – The Response
Development of social systems	5	Behavioural –the Response

Each system is briefly reviewed below in terms of its unique disturbances and imperfections and the responses that these have invoked. Also outlined is the operating system that guides and governs each system. Imperfection plays an important role in relation to operating systems, a role that will be explored in the following chapter.

A Model of a Multiverse

The theory that there are millions of universes continues to gain ground in science. Quantum physicists believe that there are multiple

John Grisham
The Racketeer.

Colin Dexter
Morse Detective

dlr

...untae County Council

Borrower Receipt

Customer name: **Mr Bernard Fitzpatrick**

Title: Morse's greatest mystery and other

08/14

Total items: 1
29/07/2014 15:12
Checked out: 3
Overdue: 0
Hold requests: 0
Ready for pickup: 0

Items that you already have on lo

Title: Traitor's kiss the life of Richard Brinsley Sher
Due: 21/08/14

Title: Racketeer
Due: 09/08/14

Thank you for using the self service system.

parallel universes and that a particle such as an electron could exist in all at the same time but in a different state. Lee Smolin has suggested that universes generate offspring like living organisms, creating universes that resemble the parent, but subject to random variation.

These theories may never be proven as science has no access to these alternative universes. Its tools can access only our own spacetime. Each other universe must have its own distinct spacetime, laws and system memory. All indicators point to these being randomly generated, yielding a diversity of universes. One of these, perhaps only one, has all the very special characteristics that are needed to support life. It may have evolved by trial and error. This is the one we inhabit and to which we are confined.

Formation of our Universe

Immediately after the Big Bang, our own universe was smooth and uniform. Quickly the initial smoothness was lost and the universe became lumpy. As the universe expanded, the lumps evolved into galaxies, creating imbalances across the universe. The *mover* behind the initial disturbance is still a matter of conjecture.

The responses to the imbalances came from the laws of nature – physics, thermodynamics and quantum mechanics. These acted as the operating system that determined the behaviour of all the heavenly bodies. Again their origin is a matter of conjecture. Under their guidance, structures of increasing complexity evolved, such as worlds and living organisms. The formation of structures needs a variety of diversified components with which to build. Imperfection was the basic mechanism that generated these components.

Evolution

The Theory of Evolution can be restated in terms of an imperfection-driven system. The whole cycle of life is dependent on errors and random mutations. Organisms emerge with constantly changing sets of traits and characteristics. Some of these traits enhance the success of the organism; others threaten this success.

The responses to these mutations come from the environment. Natural selection filters out the good traits from the bad ones and the result is the marvellous kingdom of living things.

The control mechanism of life is contained within the nucleus of the living cell. From there are issued instructions as to how to build and maintain a living organism.

Development of Tools and Devices

From the beginning, nature created man with many physical and mental imperfections. They are part of his inheritance and he has had to exercise his intellect to find ways and means to compensate. To this end, he has created tools and devices of every conceivable kind to help him on his way.

There is a never-ending stream of new human needs, driven by many powerful forces – the innate need to possess things, a consumer society that exploits this need, the trend to replace every kind of manual and mental task by machines and real needs in the fields of medicine, water supply and food supply.

Responses have come from the intellect in the form of invention, imagination, inspiration and genius. The need-to-have and the ability to invent are deeply embedded in our mental makeup. They have resulted is a bewildering array of tools and devices.

The marketplace is the filtering mechanism. A good device meets a real need; a poor one is quickly discarded.

The Conceptual Repertoire

The need-to-know is an essential characteristic of consciousness. Man has always battled against the unknown, the unpredictable, the hidden and the mysterious. These arise from his uncertain environment and they represent a threat to him.

Man's responses to his uncertain environment were earlier analysed under seven headings: *understand-model-master-exploit-interpret-realign-escape*. These responses gave rise to the disciplines of science, mathematics, art and philosophy. Each discipline has developed its own set of standards. Science, for example, uses the scientific method to adjudicate on the validity of any new scientific theory. The intellect has thus evolved different sets of tools to filter out the good from the bad.

The operating system is human consciousness and the system memory is the conceptual repertoire, the library of civilisation. The cycle commences with a new concept, continues with its propagation, and finishes when a flaw emerges that necessitates its replacement.

The Internet

The internet is an example of a self-organising system. Nobody is in charge of it. There is no master plan. Nobody knows where it will go next, just as nobody could have predicted where it is now.

It grows incrementally and achieves astonishing complexity and functionality. It does not have any particular destination, yet it is creating an entirely new social world. Its sum is far greater than the sum of its parts, many of which are quite trivial. Systems such as Facebook, Twitter and Google have unwittingly hit a resonance with some unrealised global need.

A disturbance is any new addition to the net made by some random contributor, or a new application made available. The disturbance may be useful or not. Usefulness in this context probably means:

It provides faster and more accurate access to information.

It allows for easy and efficient inter-personal communication, and

It meets a deep-felt social need to be connected.

Responses come from the global population of Internet users. They decide what is useful or not; they can press the *like* or *don't like* button on any item. Unwanted material remains on the net but is not accessed by anyone. This is equivalent to death in an information system.

There are few rules in the system. Anybody can upload anything as long as it is not ruled as socially offensive. The limitation is technical rather than behavioural. The internet shows the power of a self-organisation, a lesson learned by nature many millions of years ago.

Social Systems

Disturbances in human society arise from human frailty in the form of crime and anti-social behaviour. They can also come from society itself in the form of injustice, inequality and repression.

The response to human frailty is to design restraining systems in the form of laws, social conventions and religious guidelines. One can envisage a *system manual* that records all the categories of response that have emerged to date. Its chapters include the rules of good social behaviour, the law libraries of the world and the teachings of the religions.

Social systems are in general guided by principles such as justice, fairness, liberty and equality. Their aim is to promote the common good, often at the expense of the individual. The common good at times overrides individual liberty. Collectively, people are prepared to forego major restrictions on their personal freedom in order to remain connected with their fellow man.

Development of social systems follows the imperfection-driven model. The *mover*, the source of the initial disturbances, is man's flawed nature. The *shaker*, which initiates the responses, is human society as it attempts to legislate for the common good. The guiding system consists of the prevailing principles of social science and social justice.

Building Blocks

The systems outlined above all display a number of common characteristics.

They are imperfection driven
They are based on a cycle of birth, growth, decay and death
There is a mechanism for the creation of diversity
There is a filtering mechanism that selects the good from the bad

There is a system memory to pass on information to the next cycle.

Once started, they are self-organising.

The end product is logical in retrospect, but is not predictable or reproducible.

They sum is greater than the sum of the parts.

Imperfection driven systems are thus important building blocks of our universe. They cover not just the physical world but also the living world and the world of the mind. They are self-organising except where there is human intervention. There is an operating system that guides each system, often towards some unknown destination.

Self Organising Systems

The model for imperfection-driven systems is very similar to that which is often applied to self-organising systems.

Many systems behave as if there is a hidden purpose behind them but there may in fact be none. Self-organising systems proceed step by step with no fixed destination. The end result is logical in retrospect but unpredictable in advance. One of the big mysteries is how chaotic systems, behaving totally randomly, can still produce systems of extraordinary order and complexity. The system gradually improves due to the conservation of all the good disturbances. It becomes more complex and sophisticated. Only now is science and mathematics catching up with this phenomenon and beginning to build models of how this actually happens.

The theory of self-organising systems incorporates the idea that the internal dynamics of a system can tend to increase the inherent order and complexity of the system without any external intervention. The basic concept is that all things tend to organise themselves into patterns. Self-organising systems can build quite complex structures from simple beginnings. They are found in physics, chemistry, biology, economics and human cultures. Some examples are:

> The Market Economy
>
> Colonies of ants, bees and termites
>
> Flocking behaviour (birds, fish)
>
> Human Cultures

The internet is largely self-organising, as are online encyclopedias such as Wikipedia where there is no central editorial control. Some concepts related to self-organisation are *self-assembly, emergence and agent-based models.*

Self-assembly

This is a term used to describe processes in which a disordered system of pre-existing components forms an organised structure or pattern as a consequence of local interactions among the components themselves, without external direction. There are examples of molecular self-assembly in bio-chemistry and the technique is used to build very small electronic components in nanotechnology.

Emergence

Emergence is the rise of a system that cannot be predicted or explained from previous conditions. In evolution, the emergence of new species like the tiger is an example. Though grounded in the conditions of previous stages, its emergence could not in any way have been predicted from these conditions. Many social systems arise in exactly the same way. The transition from intelligence to consciousness is a further example.

Agent Based Models

A key notion here is that simple behavioural rules can generate complex social systems. The models simulate the actions and interactions of multiple autonomous agents, with a view to assessing their effects on the system as a whole. The system behaviour emerges as a result of interactions between individual behaviours. In the model presented above, if one imagines the *mover* and the *shaker* as two different people, one arrives at a model of two agents acting autonomously, with their interaction determining system behaviour. Examples occur in political and economic systems.

Operating Systems

All systems proceed by some set of rules and procedures. There is a local operating system that manages the system and guides it towards its destination. It provides the logic of the system

The physical world has the laws of nature.

The living world has DNA and RNA, the control system of the living cell.

The mental world has consciousness, the control system of human intelligence.

Within these major categories, there are many smaller operating systems, as for example the organisation of a beehive or of a busy office. Operating systems may be invisible and intangible, but they exert a powerful influence. Without them, systems would fall into chaos.

Computer Operating System

At technical level, the various operating systems appear to have much in common with the operating system of a computer. Every desktop computer, tablet, and smartphone incorporates an operating system (OS) that provides functionality for the device. The OS is the device's brain. It consists of a set of specialised computer programs, performing many functions such as:

Accepting instructions from the user via a keyboard or tactile screen

Loading and executing application programs such as word processing

Managing all the hardware resources such as disc storage, monitors and memory

Allowing a number of applications to run simultaneously, sharing the same resources

Handling various error situations

Well known examples are Microsoft's WINDOWS and Apple's IOS. Windows was designed originally by Bill Gates in the 1980's and has been in continual development ever since. Some hundreds of skilled man-years have gone into its development.

A Cosmic Operating System

One could infer the existence of a cosmic operating system that supervises and synchronises the millions of multiple universes, and the major systems that exist within these universes. It would preside over all cosmic cycles of birth, evolution and eventual death. It must reside externally. Plato would have said that it resides in the Locus.

In the next chapter, this idea is explored further.

Chapter 10.
THE THEORY OF C-OS

From the examples in the previous chapter, three important kingdoms emerge – the inanimate, the animate and the conscious. Viewing their operation, a consistent pattern can be discerned. One could conclude that the purpose of any kingdom is to generate the seed from which the next kingdom will develop. The inanimate world took 9 billion years to develop the seed from which the living world emerged. This is turn took 4 billion years to develop the seed from which consciousness emerged. There is thus a slow cycle of kingdom creation, within which local cycles operate for the specific purpose of seed generation.

This observation enables a new theory to be put forward -The Theory of C-OS. This deals with the formation of new kingdoms under the control of a cosmic operating system which will be called C-OS.

Within each kingdom, imperfection carries the responsibility for preparing any kingdom for the emergence of the next one. Its cycle of trial and error leads to ever increasing complexity and sophistication until the right combination is eventually found and a seed develops that is ready for transition. The transition itself is not demonstrably a function of imperfection but imperfection has done all the groundwork and prepared everything in advance. Without its action no progeny would have taken been born - the kingdom would have remained sterile forever.

The Cycles of C-OS

The theory envisages two interacting cycles as follows:

The Cosmic Cycle

A new kingdom emerges.

The Local Cycle

Imperfection starts its work cycle.

Disturbances and imbalances occur.

Filters react to select to sort out the good from the bad.

Diversity increases. More complex structures evolve.

New imperfections appear.

Transition

The seed of the next kingdom emerges.

There is a giant leap in functionality.

The next cosmic cycle begins.

The diagram below illustrates the process. The three known kingdoms are shown, together with a hypothetical 4th kingdom. Within each there are interlocking sub-cycles.

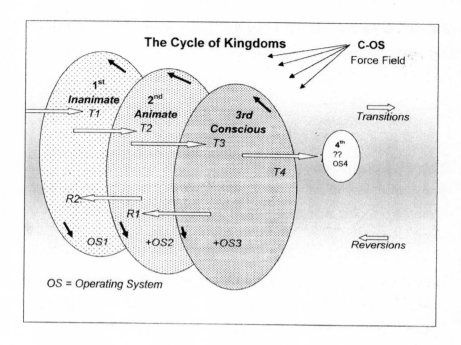

The diagram shows four kingdoms- 1st, 2nd, 3rd and the hypothetical 4th, each with its own operating system. Under certain conditions, an entity can cross the boundaries, either forwards or backwards. Four forward transitions are shown:

:

T1	From nothing to animate	TheBig Bang
T2.	From inanimate to animate	The first living cell
T3.	From animate to Conscious	Homo Sapiens
T4	From conscious to post-conscious	The 4th Kingdom?

Two backward reversions are shown:

R1	From conscious to animate	Loss of consciousness
R2	From animate to inanimate	Death of an organism

A forward transition is rare and complex. A backward reversion is easy and frequent. Death is a reversion from the living to the inanimate. All the kingdoms co-exist; three are found simultaneously in man.

Key Concepts
C-OS

There is a cosmic operating system C-OS which provides guidance and control for the entire cosmos. It does this through some kind of force field that is active everywhere. Everything resides within this force field.

Under C-OS, three known kingdoms operate. There may be others, past, present and future that we do not know anything about. C-OS Theory is intended to apply also to kingdoms that are not observable, perhaps a kingdom prior to the Big Bang and future possible kingdoms.

Kingdoms

Each kingdom is a self-organising cycle. Once in motion the cycle does not need any external inputs to keep it going. The cycles give the impression of having a purpose, but self-organising systems do not have a fixed destination. They are a process rather than a directed journey.

Imperfection

The evolution of each kingdom is driven by flaws, imbalances and disturbances. These gives rise to responses and thus generate the diversity and complexity. Their function is to prepare for transition to a higher-level kingdom.

Operating Systems

Each kingdom is driven by its own unique operating system, OS. This must be linked to C-OS, to ensure that the OS of all kingdoms are synchronised with each other. Even man-made operating systems are the products of an intelligence which, under C-OS theory, is itself under the guidance of C-OS.

The transition from one kingdom to another involves the introduction of a new level of operating system. The components and configurations remain the same but now they are managed in a totally different way. There is a quantum leap in functionality.

Structures

The kingdom cycle results in a steadily increasing complexity and functionality both of components and structures. The building of structures needs a diversity of components, each carrying out specialised functions; for example, the many specialised components of a Swiss watch. A set of totally uniform components needs no arrangement and organisation and thus can yield no functionality.

At some point, perhaps after billions of cycles, a structure of unique character emerges that has special properties that are instantly recognised by C-OS. This is the seed of the next kingdom. It is proposed here that a kind of *resonance* takes place between the structure and C-OS, like a tuning fork suddenly vibrating in harmony with a prevailing sound. As a result, the structure now behaves in a totally different way.

Resonance

Musicians use a tuning fork to give them the precise pitch of an important note such as middle-C on a piano. The tuning fork has a natural frequency and it vibrates at this frequency - 440 beats per second in the case of middle-C. If a strong note of this precise frequency occurs in its vicinity, the tuning fork will start to vibrate. It resonates to the sound. One could say that the inert piece of metal become *alive*. It may even feel *good* as it feels in perfect harmony with its environment!

In a radio there is a tuning circuit, usually composed of an inductance and a capacitance. One can vary the value of the capacitance by turning the tuning knob, thus changing the natural frequency of the circuit. At different frequencies, the radio can be tuned to receive transmissions from different stations, each of which has its own allotted frequency for transmission.

For this to work, a few things have to be in place. There has to be an external signal which is transmitted at a given frequency. The components of the receiver have to be arranged in the form of a tuning circuit which can resonate with the incoming signal. The remaining circuitry amplifies this resonance and conveys it to the loudspeakers.

Imagine a child playing with a radio. The child really does not know what a radio is for. It plays around randomly with the knobs. Imagine its amazement when suddenly the radio produces magnificent music. It is the same radio but now it is transformed into something else. As a small silent box, it had practically zero functionality. Now it has magnificent functionality. The box is relaying a concert live from Sydney!

It is convenient to imagine that seed of a new kingdom contains some form of tuning circuit that allows it to tune into some higher functionality within C-OS.

As a thought experiment, imagine that there is a cosmic transmitter that sends out signals at a range of specific frequencies. One of the signals is the *life signal*. There are on earth billions of clumps of inanimate matter. Imperfection has played around with these, producing millions of different permutations and combinations - somewhat like the child playing with the radio. Suddenly one of these clumps takes the form of a tuning circuit that can resonate with the life signal. Magically it becomes alive! The transition does not require any specific action on anyone's part. It is a random, quasi-accidental, synchronisation of two independent entities.

Where does C-OS reside?

Scientists sometimes refer to our universe as spacetime. It is a place governed by the laws of physics and where the maximum speed is the speed of light. Anything outside of spacetime does not have to obey the same laws or observe the maximum speed-limit. For C-OS to operate as suggested, it has to reside outside spacetime. This is now scientifically acceptable. A number of natural phenomena appear to have components outside spacetime, especially in the area of quantum mechanics.

Scientists use the term local in relation to any events that occur within spacetime and non-local in relation to those which appear to act from outside.

The argument has now come full circle. One is back with Plato and his ideas of the Locus. To Plato all the laws and abstract concepts of the universe resided in the Locus. The Locus predated the universe and was external to it. He postulated that our minds had special access to these laws and concepts, and developed his doctrine of recollection to account for how this could happen. C-OS theory agrees in part with Plato's theory, but suggests an entirely different mechanism as to how our minds are tuned into the Locus or its equivalent.

Master/Slave Systems

One speaks about the laws of physics as if they were resident in matter. Similarly about consciousness, as if it were resident in the human brain. This may not be true. Any system can be controlled remotely. There are many examples in the computer world.

The operating system of a computer can take control of a remote computer and appear as if were physically present there. All that this needs is a communication channel and a piece of master-slave software to be installed on the local machine. Perhaps this is also nature's way. The laws of physics may not be resident in matter, but elsewhere, doing their work remotely. The operating system that controls our thought sequences may similarly be resident elsewhere. It just appears to us to be local.

There are many technical advantages to this kind of arrangement. Lower-level kingdom-specific tasks and data are kept locally, while higher-level tasks, applicable to multiple kingdoms, are controlled centrally. Minimal intelligence is thus required at the local end. This is the solution for maximum efficiency, economy and simplicity. Intuitively one feels that it is the solution that nature would adopt. Nature avoids redundancy and duplication.

This logic leaves C-OS as the central guidance system of the universe. Matter, life, minds – these operate under a combination of local and remote operating systems.

A logical divide of function would appear to be along Gödelian lines, Gödelian functions being carried out locally and non Gödelian functions coming under remote control.

Gödelian functions are rule-based, determinate and predictable. They can be replicated by computer. For matter, they could be the laws of physics; for life, homeostatic tasks such as blood temperature control; for the mind, routine computation and logic.

Non-Gödelian functions cannot be reduced to a set of rules. They are non-predictable, intuitive and often mysterious. For matter, they could be the strange behaviour of quantum mechanics; for life, they could be interpretative and managerial operations of RNA; for the mind, they could be qualities such as imagination, intuition and virtue. In making a divide such as this, nature may have anticipated Gödel by some billions of years.

It is initially a scary thought that the rules guiding our conscious processes are actually under the control of a remote system whose presence we cannot even detect. Yet on reflection, it holds out immense possibilities and casts a totally different light on human individuality and free will.

A novel theory such as C-OS inevitably invites many questions, both scientific and philosophic.

> Is it good or bad science?
> How does it relate to Theories of Everything?
> How does it relate to current religious beliefs?
> What does it say about creation?
> Is it leading anywhere, or is it on a random course?

Science
Good or bad Science?

One cannot prove the existence of a force such as C-OS, but many of the theories currently being put forward in cosmology are far from being proven. In quantum physics, there is much talk of alternative universes, to which we have no means of access.

The Theory of Evolution is at times not accepted as a fully legitimate scientific theory, as one cannot test it in a laboratory or make any verifiable predictions with it. Nevertheless it provides such a good retro-fit for so much that has happened in the past that few now dispute it validity. C-OS theory is also a retro-fit for much that has happened in the past. One cannot make predictions as to where it will lead next, but a broad sense of direction can be discerned.

Quantum Theory

In quantum mechanics, two particles frequently communicate with each other to synchronise their actions. If the interaction takes place within spacetime, it is deemed *local*, i.e. the particles can communicate with each other with the speed of light. An interaction called entanglement occurs where the interaction between the two particles takes place instantly, even if the particles are a whole universe apart. The action is deemed *non-local*. There is no scientific explanation as to how this can happen. It is taken by some scientists as an indication of another operating system at play, one from outside spacetime that is controlling the synchronisation of the two particles.

Paradoxes also arise in the role of the observer. It appears that a particle has no particular properties until it is measured, following which it randomly sets certain properties based on probabilities. So the observer is deeply entangled in the behaviour of the particle. This entanglement has reopened much debate about the exact nature of free will. Some maintain that it is an illusion, that our actions and those of the particles have been preordained since the beginning of time.

Paradoxes like these lead many to believe that quantum theory is incomplete and may be missing a component, one that resides perhaps outside conventional spacetime.

Incompleteness

Gödel's Theory of Incompleteness deals with the mental models we create to describe the universe. Since these are part of the universe, as we ourselves are, our understandings are the system modelling itself. The models are thus self-referential and unverifiable in an absolute sense. If however the mind is linked to a logic from outside spacetime, the self-referential limitation disappears. We can be more certain of our mental models.

Mathematics

Plato thought deeply about the mystery of mathematics. Nature appears to obey beautiful, elegant mathematical laws and equations. The human mind is able to discover these equations and use them to model and predict nature. So much so that for many scientists the equation becomes more real than nature itself. Plato asked if there lay a hidden relationship between the human mind, these equations and nature itself.

Under C-OS theory, the laws of physics are specific to the kingdom of matter; they are local and are thus contained within the local OS. However their origin lies in C-OS. The way matter decodes these laws and obeys them is mysterious and belongs within C-OS. The human mind, in inventing mathematics is using abstraction, imagination, judgment and understanding – qualities that are within the domain of C-OS. So the three entities - matter, equations and mind - are linked and synchronised within C-OS and are thus part of the same thing.

Theory of Everything

Scientific Theories of Everything (TOE) deal exclusively with nature and the behaviour of the physical world. They start with the fundamental particles of which atoms are made and work up from there. They are essentially bottom-up. They do not attempt to include the living world or the world of the human mind within the same framework. Only religions do this.

In the grand scheme of creation, there are *things* like water and rocks, living *organisms* like the butterfly, *persons* like us, *intelligence* and *consciousness* and the complex *processes* or guidance systems that control all this. Looking at all the main entities, it is *processes* that must take precedence. They are powerful, intelligent and had to precede everything else. They permeate every grain of sand, every butterfly, every person and every thought. Everything obeys their dictates and moves according to their plan. Things, organisms, people, ideas, intelligence and consciousness are just transients along the path of the processes. They come and go. If the human race disappeared tomorrow, the processes would continue on their majestic way. The same applies to the disappearance of any of the other transients.

A true TOE should therefore start with processes rather than with a single transient. It should aim to unify the dynamics of matter, life and thought into a single cohesive framework. The C-OS vision of the cosmos is a top-down one, based on systems theory. It starts with ideas of a cosmic control system and works down from there. It lies somewhere between the religious and the scientific world views.

Philosophy

C-OS theory has echoes in some of the philosophic concepts of earlier chapters..

Plato

Plato's Theory of Forms was outlined in Chapter 2 / Plato. It deals with the same entities as C-OS Theory, but differs in many significant ways. A dialogue between Plato and C-OS might run as follows:

P.   The physical world is imperfect.

C.   *Agreed.*

P.   One can reach perfection through the intellect.

C.   *No. The intellect is part of the world and flawed also.*

P.   The human intellect is supreme.

C.   *No. It is just another imperfection-driven kingdom.*
        The other kingdoms are of equal importance.

P.   Concepts like justice are eternal and immutable.

C.   *No. They change and decay like everything else.*

P.   There is a duality in the universe between the physical and the conceptual.

C.   *The duality is between the local and the non-local,*
     i.e. what originates inside spacetime and what originates outside it.

P.   There is duality in man: body v. mind/soul

C.   *The duality is between the non-local operating systems that guide him both physically and mentally and the local products of these systems.*

P.   The universe it at base perfection-driven.

C.   *No. It is imperfection-driven.*

Religions

Taoism teaches that all parts of the universe are in harmony and human beings are part of this harmony. TAO is the unified something from which all things arise. It is beyond the reach of intellectual knowledge. It pervades the natural world, constantly ordering and nurturing it. It is always present. Goodness lies in living in harmony with TAO. Death is just one of nature's transformations from one state to another.

Hinduism teaches that all reality – gods, plants, animals, the physical universe and humans – share a common essence which is called Brahmin. The universe has a cyclical pattern undergoing long periods of creation and destruction, a rhythmic pattern that repeats itself endlessly. Within this cyclical pattern each individual is also created and re-created repeatedly until final release is attained. Liberation is an experience characterized by infinite being, infinite awareness and infinite bliss. Reincarnation occurs into many different life forms – human, animal, plant, gods, goddesses and demons.

De Chardin
De Chardin wrote as follows in 1935:[62]

> The Cosmos is a dynamic entity in process. Each element of the Cosmos is woven from all the others. There is a collective unity bonded by energy. Evolution is an ascent towards higher and higher complexity and consciousness. From the cell to the thinking animal, a process of psychical concentration leads to consciousness.

---

[62] *Pierre Teilhard De **Chardin**, 1881-1955*. French Jesuit, Palaeontologist and Philosopher, *The Phenomenon of Man, 1955*

Evolution will culminate in the Omega Point, a state of supreme consciousness. The noosphere is the collective consciousness of humanity, the network of thoughts and emotions that connects us all. Eventually it will culminate in a stupendous thinking machine. The Omega Point existed from the beginning of the cosmos and is the cause for its growth in complexity and consciousness. It is the parallel of a godhead that draws everything unto itself.

Imperfection exists in mankind by virtue of its being in the process of becoming. The point of the cosmos is to achieve multi-dimensional wholeness. Humanity is part and parcel of this progression towards wholeness.

A recurring concept in all the above is the achievement of harmony, right across all creation. Perhaps the fundamental concept lying behind all of C-OS is also that of *harmony*.

Creation

The Theory of C-OS has obvious implications relating to creation theory.

It could be TAO, the eternal, unseen force that is the origin and order of the universe.

It could be Brahmin, the universal spirit that is the origin and essence of all creation, and that controls its multiple cycles.

It could have been created by the omnipotent, personal God of western religions as His mechanism of creation, but the omnipresence of imperfection would present many difficulties. Also the idea of man as a transient along the way would not sit very comfortably.

It could be an intelligent design mechanism, but it is not consistent with intermittent, random interventions in the process of creation

C-OS theory does not answer the creation debate, but it may move it back a step. It envisages an inexorable process of unknown origin which existed before actual creation began.

Purpose

Perfection implies purpose; there is a specific destination to be reached. If perfection is dropped as an ideal, then purpose also can be dropped. Imperfection does not have a purpose. Rather it is a movement away from the status quo. It proceeds stepwise in this fashion. It aims to become something better, but has no long-term vision of what that might be.

What we witness in the universe is a very extraordinary *process*, a process of continual creation. Perhaps this is its real purpose. It is the journey, not the destination that matters.

Individual purpose is different from cosmic purpose. It is essential for people to feel a purpose to their lives. Taoism seeks perfect harmony with TAO; Hinduism seeks liberation from the cycle of reincarnation; Christians seeks redemption and final reward in Heaven. Each sees a different connection between personal and cosmic purpose. Christianity infers at times that the cosmos is designed to support the purposes of man. Eastern religions teach the reverse – the purpose of the individual is to support the cosmos.

A Fourth Kingdom

The logic of C-OS leads one to believe that a fourth transition is inevitable. Imperfection is probably working on it right now.

It will likely be a very long task. Preparation for the 2nd kingdom - the animate - took 9 billion years (=3 squared). Preparation of the 3rd kingdom – the conscious – took 4 billion years (=2 squared). Assuming some kind of geometrical progression, one might deduce that preparation for the 4th kingdom (the post-conscious) might take 1 billion years (=1 squared). Homo Sapiens appeared some 200,000 years ago, so this would leave some 800,000 years still to run. The kingdom of the conscious still has plenty of time to get its act together!

Again using the logic of C-OS, one can say a few things about a 4th kingdom:

> It will emerge from consciousness, currently the kingdom of highest functionality. The main task of preparation will be to achieve harmony within the present kingdom. Progress from a conflict-ridden, divided kingdom does not feel aesthetically or intellectually acceptable. De Chardin has surmised that human evolution is heading for an Omega Point where all conflicts will be finally resolved. The 4th transition may be a step along the way.

> An entirely new level of functionality will emerge. What this might be is impossible to envisage. It will be still under the control of C-OS but at a much higher level.

The transition may well arise from the synchronisation of many different consciousnesses to yield complex new structures unthought-of at the present time. Concepts such as individuality and freewill will probably undergo radical transformation, as C-OS assumes a higher level of control.

Why Imperfection?

Perfection does not play any visible role in C-OS processes. Instead it is imperfection that lies at the heart of these. It is the workshop of creation. In this workshop, the tiger was forged.

Why was imperfection chosen to play such a pivotal role? A few clues might be:

It is continuous. Its cycle of creation can go on forever. It is not once-off.

It demands participation from the players involved. They are not spectators.

It does not require specific goals and destinations. It is open-ended.

How was the choice actually made? We simply do not know. We may have to pass through a few more transitions before we find out.

Chapter 11.
LIVING WITH IMPERFECTION

Accepting that we ourselves and all that is around us are imperfection-driven entities, how should we respond? If we follow this somewhat unsettling idea through to its logical conclusion, how must we realign our ideas? Are we capable of making such a realignment? Could we find some kind of liberation in these new ideas? Have we a fatal flaw that could yet destroy us?

The new scenario clearly has implications at many different levels – intellectual, personal, societal, artistic, religious and behavioural.

Realignment
Intellectual

Since the time of Plato, we have followed the path of determinism. We have inhabited a world where purpose, design, order and destination have ruled. This world has been created over thousands of years by our own intellect. To substitute it now with one where chance, randomness, and absence of specific purpose and destination prevail – this requires a substantial mental leap.

Unknowingly perhaps, we have already begun to make this leap. Scientists are now well used to dealing with a world like this, and many cannot conceive of any other. Artists, always sensitive to the winds of change, have begun to reflect it in their art. In human institutions, the big monolithic structures of the past are beginning to crumble. In society we are slowly coming to terms with ever-increasing diversity. In our approach to religion, more individuality and freedom of thought are evident. Behaviourally we are beginning to reassess our relationship with nature and to realise that a profound change may be needed here also.

Personal Lives

To look at television is to be bombarded with images of perfection - the perfect face, the perfect figure, the perfect house etc. Business has discovered the marketability of perfection. Perfection is available at the touch of a button, but of course it comes with a price.

> *The thing that is really hard, and really amazing, is giving up on being perfect and beginning the work of becoming yourself.*
>
> - Anna Quindlen[63]

> *Imperfection is beauty, madness is genius and it's better to be absolutely ridiculous than absolutely boring.*
>
> - Marilyn Monroe
>
> Interpreted as: If you follow society's convention in terms of appearance and normality, you may fit in, but you will lose individuality and a sense of self. It is better to be unusual,

---

[63] Anna Marie **Quindlen,** 1952-. American author/journalist, Pulitzer Prize for Commentary 1992, *Being Perfect*

an outcast, or hated, than to be mediocre, for you will surely
never be remembered by fitting in.

*We are all wonderful, beautiful wrecks. That's what connects us-
-that we're all broken, all beautifully imperfect.*

- Emilio Estevez[64]

The world isn't Eden, it's never just right
But a life fully lived, it's an earthly delight   *- Marcia Wrixon*[65]

We should enjoy the unpredictability of life and nature for its own
sake and not regard it as some kind of error or mistake. We could
gear ourselves to handle unpredictability better, rather than trying
to eliminate it from our lives altogether, a quite impossible task. We
should avoid the beaten tracks and search out the new ones.

Beaten tracks are for beaten men - a poster in a nearby gym

Society
In the modern world there is widespread resistance to conformity,
particularly among young people. They do not accept institutions of
the past which were based on conformity and authority. New social
systems are needed to allow for diversity, experiment, personal liberty
and dissent. Nature has been able to handle such systems with
success, so perhaps we can learn from it how to do the same. We have
seen how independent agents acting randomly and in self-interest can

[64] Emilio **Estevez**, Actor: The Breakfast Club. The eldest son of Martin Sheen and
      Janet Sheen Estevez was born on May 12, 1962, in New York City

[65] Marcia **Wrixon**, Irish Poet, living in Kinsale, Co. Cork *Love is for the Birds*

still lead to well-ordered systems, given the right set of filters. We need positive filters, ones that promote responsibility within diversity, rather than negative responses of exclusion and punishment.

In society we have the old, the sick, the handicapped, the addicted and the deviant. These are not deviations from some arbitrary societal norm. They are part of the human diversity of which we all are part. They are just as beautiful as everybody else. It is only our inherited warped thinking that tells us otherwise.

There is nothing either good or bad but thinking made it so. [66]

- Hamlet

Religions

The new trends have deep implications for many religions. Some have found difficulty in coping with evolution theory. It appeared to cut across their own long-held beliefs regarding the origins of man. Many followers have by now succeeded in reconciling the apparent conflicts, but pockets of intense resistance remain.

More and more people are benefiting from the fruits of science and technology and are becoming more scientifically literate. They are increasingly prepared to accept the apparently random chain of events that led to the creation of our world and the emergence of man. There is a move away from the isms of the past. These are being replaced by new isms such as *capitalism, materialism, multiculturalism, egalitarianism, liberalism, and humanism.* Diversity rather than conformity is the basis of this new world.

---

[66] **Shakespeare**, *Hamlet*

People are seeking more individual freedom and choice of life style. Authority is being questioned as never before. Religions need to realign themselves with this new reality, or else they too run the risk of being swept away.

Man and Nature

We are not apart from nature. We came from the same dust cloud. It is not our enemy. We do not need to defeat it or escape from it by every means possible. At death, we return to the dust cloud.

> *A human being is part of the whole called by us universe, a part limited in time and space. We experience ourselves, our thoughts and feelings as something separate from the rest. A kind of optical delusion of consciousness. This delusion is a kind of prison for us, restricting us to our personal desires and to affection for a few persons nearest to us. Our task must be to free ourselves from the prison by widening our circle of compassion to embrace all living creatures and the whole of nature in its beauty. The true value of a human being is determined by the measure and the sense in which they have obtained liberation from the self. We shall require a substantially new manner of thinking if humanity is to survive.*
>
> - Einstein[67]

The Fatal Flaw

In ancient Greek drama, the hero always performed wondrous deeds. But he also had a fatal flaw, such as Achilles' heel. In the end it was this flaw that brought about his downfall. We can ask

---

[67]   Letter of 1950, as quoted in the New York Times 29 March 1972

concerning man: *Has he also a fatal flaw, one likely to bring about his eventual destruction?*

If there is such a flaw, our reasoning so far would lead us to conclude that it must be the flaw that upsets most the delicate balances of nature that have brought us into existence and continue to support us. We are seriously interfering with nature and may be destroying the response mechanisms it has developed over billions of years.

> We interfere with the DNA of plants, of animals, and shortly we suspect of human beings as well. This is interfering with the life force itself at its most fundamental level.

> We pollute the atmosphere and the oceans in a potentially irreversible way. Nature's responses no longer work; they cannot cope with disturbances on the present scale.

> We regard the resources of nature, such as oil and minerals, as inexhaustible commodities, things to be exploited as quickly as possible in our race for power, possessions and control.

> We use advanced technology, such as nuclear power, as an instrument of war and destruction. It may rebound on us one day.

> We are forcing nature into formal moulds for which it was never designed.

> We are ruining the bio-diversity which has brought us such a wealth of essential foods and remedies.

Carl Sagan's view that all high-technology civilisations are inherently self-destructive may well be true. Man could be on such a self-destructive course, and it is difficult to envisage any mechanism by which the brakes can be applied. The forces against restraint are too powerful - exponential population growth, global demands for ever higher standards of living, the economic imperative for continuous growth, manipulation of resources to support political power, and the view of nature as a source of personal wealth. No counter-force, however well-meaning, can withstand such an array of opposition. A massive realignment is needed, but it would need a new messiah to lead it. Religions that regard the world either as an enemy or as a gift to man are not in a position to offer any solutions.

The fatal flaw is therefore a complete disconnection from nature, driven by an intellect that feels that it and its demands reign supreme. The real enemy is not the world. It is the human need to possess, control and exploit the world.

Liberation

Acceptance of the imperfection implicit in all creation and abandonment of our constant search for perfection is a form of liberation that can give us a new sense of freedom. We can be freed from the constant, futile search for perfection and the guilt we feel if we do not achieve it in our personal lives, spiritual lives, environment and intellectual pursuits. We will reject isms that force us into conformity, such as communism, fascism, racism and consumerism. We will abandon the idea of a world that has the purpose and precision of a Swiss watch where determinism and predictability rule. We need to shed the belief that the unexpected - adversity, chance and accident - is just an unwanted departure from some imaginary ideal world; that God somehow intended the world to be something better than it really is, but that something went wrong along the way. We will stop thinking that we are something apart from nature, own it, and are its masters; that nature was made for us and that somehow we can eventually escape from it. Finally we must realize that our own intellect is not supreme and flawless and that it is not the only route towards ultimate truth.

The New Age

It would appear that intellectually we are passing through a long transition phase. The Age of Perfection is dying and is being slowly replaced by the Age of Imperfection. The transition can be said to have begun with new concept of evolution and continues to this day. Imperfection is spreading. There are many areas where concepts of perfection and conformity still reign and are enforced, but instinct tells us that they too will yield in time to the new perspective.

The Age of Perfection has left us with a wonderful heritage - the music of Mozart, the paintings of Caravaggio, the science of Newton, the beautiful cathedrals of the world, and a deep reservoir of moral codes. These will remain with us, but will never be replicated. Their wellsprings have dried up.

Alongside this heritage one must line up the negatives. Greatest among these is the fundamentalism that sometimes followed the pursuit of perfection and conformity, whether political, religious or scientific. Those who became owners and guardians of *The Truth* often abused their power. The passing of this type of fundamentalism will not be regretted.

The Era of Imperfection will bring many benefits. Its acceptance of diversity as a fundamental law of nature will make many of the isms of the past redundant. Individual freedom of choice and action will take centre stage. Our societies will have to be based on tolerance rather than elitism. A new music and new theatre will emerge, breaking all the rules of form and shape inherited from the past.

There will also be negatives. Many of the moral compasses of the past will be lost. Each person will want to invent his/her own moral code and purpose in life. People will look to technology rather than religion for a solution to all their problems. An insatiable demand for materials things will replace the search for inner peace. Nature and its diversity may get destroyed in the process, and there yet might be a very high price to pay for this. Politics will become more fragmented and unstable, and societies will become more difficult to govern. Control of many elements of society may pass to big business, the masters of the new technologies. A new type of conformity could emerge, conformity to the needs of the marketplace.

A new consciousness is undoubtedly developing, supported by communications and technology. Hundreds of millions of people are now social networking. These networks are not bounded by country, society, race or creed.

One senses that a new transition is coming but we have no idea of when or what it might be. We could well be the two tramps sitting on a mound of clay in *Waiting for Godot.*

But that is not the question. Why are we here, that is the question. And we are blessed in this, that we happen to know the answer. Yes, in this immense confusion one thing alone is clear. We are waiting for Godot to come.

Chapter 12.
A PERSONAL NOTE

At this point, the faithful reader is entitled to know where the author stands in the midst of all this uncertainty. Firstly there is no such thing as being absolutely certain about anything. One gives ones provisional consent to certain ideas without any illusions about their infallibility.

The author believes in God, but remains uncertain about His exact nature. In the Age of Imperfection, such uncertainty should be quite permissible. Thomas Aquinas gave eight attributes of God - *simplicity, incomprehensibility, omnipresence, immutability, eternity, oneness, goodness* and *perfection*. The attribute of incomprehensibility would appear to infer that the other attributes cannot be defined with any great degree of confidence.

The attribute of perfection is one of those covered by the attribute of incomprehensibility. In Chapter 2, the many anomalies and paradoxes surrounding the concept of perfection were explored.

God could be a process. Certainly some extraordinary process is taking place leading the universe and everything in it towards some unimaginable place. It infuses everything. It meets many of Aquinas' attributes of God - *simplicity, incomprehensibility, omnipresence, immutability, eternity and oneness.* This process could be C-OS or the TAO or Brahmin of eastern religions.

The author does not believe his soul will live on as an independent, intelligent entity. Rather that the sublime process to which he has contributed will live on forever. His contribution may have been micro-miniscule but that does not matter.

God could be a person. In the Christian religion in which the author was reared, the concept of a personal God, with whom one can communicate and develop a personal relationship, remains a powerful influence. One cannot have the same relationship with a process. The basic teaching of Christianity, often garbled by its messengers, is as vibrant today as it was 2000 years ago:

> *A new command I give you: Love one another just as I have loved you…My peace I leave with you… My peace I give you.*

The essential attribute of this God is *goodness.* Goodness is difficult to define. Yet it is easily recognised. The author is among other things an organist. He has played in churches of different denominations and along the way has met many people of extraordinary goodness. They stand out like lighthouses. Goodness transcends all boundaries.

Ideally the author would like to have it both ways. The cosmic process can continue on its majestic way, dealing with creation and the emergence of new universes and kingdoms. One must do one's best to live in total harmony with this process. The personal God, relieved of the need to be also the all-powerful creator of everything, becomes more local and accessible. He could be the collective soul of humankind. As such, a little piece resides in each of us and we can communicate with it internally. This God can evolve with us as we head towards some unknown Omega Point.

Organised religion is a man made thing. It does not possess the right to claim absolute truth. (Neither does science.) Nevertheless it fulfils a very essential human need. It acts as a focus and platform for the innate goodness displayed by so many people.

The deepest truth about the human condition may in fact be music. We have absolutely no idea of why or how certain patterns of sound waves can reach deep into our psyche and produce such powerful emotions. Music proceeds by creating tensions through dissonances, little imperfections, and then resolving these. It is a metaphor for how the entire universe operates: *imperfection > tension > resolution*. Deep inside we recognise this.

Music and religion are mysterious and they work in the same way. Just because we cannot provide technical explanations for them does not mean that we can dismiss them. In fact, this is the reason for their power. They refuse to be measured with a measuring tape. They can thus retain their mystery.

God, in whatever form He takes, is music. He is ever creating new harmonies. Everything vibrates to these harmonies. Intelligence and consciousness can, in the course of their many ego-trips, shut out these harmonies. But in the end, the music prevails.

The author had the good fortune to be educated by Cistercian monks. To them he is eternally grateful. They taught him how, in the midst of all the noise, to listen to the harmonies.

EPILOGUE

There was a crooked man

Nobody is perfect

and he walked a crooked mile,

No such thing as a straight mile

He found a crooked sixpence

Even money is bent

upon a crooked stile.

A flawed carpenter built it

He bought a crooked cat,

The cat is flawed

which caught a crooked mouse,

So is the mouse

And they all lived together
in a little crooked house.

Somehow, we have to learn

how to all live together in this

little crooked house

INDEX

Lightning Source UK Ltd.
Milton Keynes UK
UKOW05f0458240714

235660UK00001B/23/P